W9-BJD-843

BOBBY JONES ON GOLF

Other books in the
Golf Digest Classic Series
Golf Fundamentals by Seymour Dunn
The Complete Golfer by Harry Vardon
Five Lessons by Ben Hogan
Swing the Clubhead by Ernest Jones

BOBBY JONES
ON GOLF

Robert Tyre (Bobby) Jones

Foreword by Charles Price

Illustrations by Anthony Ravielli

A Golf Digest Classics Book

Copyright © 1966 by Robert Tyre Jones, Jr.
Reprinted 1984, 1986, 1988, 1989 by Golf Digest/Tennis, Inc.
  by permission Doubleday & Co., Inc.
All rights reserved including the right of reproduction
  in whole or in part in any form.

Library of Congress: 85-30574
ISBN: 0-914178-88-1

Manufactured in the United States of America

Distributed by:
  Golf Digest/Tennis, Inc.
  A New York Times Company
  5520 Park Avenue
  Post Office Box 0395
  Trumbull, CT 06611-0395

Printing and binding by R.R. Donnelley & Sons

Library of Congress Cataloging-in-Publication Data

Jones, Bobby, 1902-1917.
  Bobby Jones on golf.

  Reprint. Originally published: Garden City, N.Y.:
Doubleday, 1966.
  "A Golf Digest classics book."
  1. Golf.   I. Title.
GV965.J6 1986   796.352'3   85-30574
ISBN 0-914178-88-1

Contents

Foreword by Charles Price   ix

Introduction   xiii

CHAPTER ONE   I

THE ULTIMATE OBJECT • SOME MEMORABLE ADVICE • THE FEEL
OF A GOLF CLUB • HOLDING THE CLUB • MAINTAINING THE "FEEL"
• THE VALUE OF GOOD FORM • SWINGING THE CLUB HEAD • HOW
FORM AFFECTS SWINGING.

CHAPTER TWO   17

EASE AND COMFORT • SHIFTING THE WEIGHT • PLACING THE FEET
• PROPER POSTURE • POSITIONING THE BALL • THE PROCEDURE IN
ADDRESSING THE BALL • VARIATIONS IN THE STANCES • STAYING IN
MOTION • THE POSITION OF THE HEAD • "REACHING" FOR THE
BALL • AN INSIDIOUS HABIT.

CHAPTER THREE   39

THE PURPOSE OF THE BACKSWING • ORIGINATING THE BACKSWING
• ARGUMENTS FOR A LONG BACKSWING • ROLL OF THE LEFT FOOT
• COCKING THE WRISTS • THE POSITION AT THE TOP • SHIFTING
THE WEIGHT.

CHAPTER FOUR 53

DEVELOPING A STYLE • THE MOST IMPORTANT MOVEMENT • AN IMPORTANT FAULT • USING THE BODY • HITTING DOWN ON THE BALL • INSIDE-OUT? • USING YOUR LEGS • LOOKING UP.

CHAPTER FIVE 69

COMMON SENSE AND SHORT SHOTS • MECHANICS OF THE PITCH • THE NATURE OF BACKSPIN • WHAT DISTINGUISHES THE CHIP • CHOOSING THE CLUB TO FIT THE SHOT • AN ESSENTIAL FOR SHORT SHOTS • THE PROPER PROCEDURE JUST OFF THE GREEN.

CHAPTER SIX 81

GETTING CONTROL • A LIGHT GRIP • LOOKING AT THE BALL • NEVER IMITATE • THE PENDULUM STROKE • METHOD • PUTTING PRACTICE • MAKING CONTACT • SHORT PUTTS • STROKE OR TAP? • APPROACH PUTTING • SPOTTING THE LINE • CHOOSING A PUTTER • ATTITUDE.

CHAPTER SEVEN 105

FINDING THE ORTHODOX • STARTING A NEW SEASON • THE STRAIGHT LEFT ARM • USING THE GROUND • STAYING DOWN TO THE BALL • TIMING • DELAYING THE HIT • CLOSED FACE VS. OPEN FACE • HITTING FROM THE INSIDE.

CHAPTER EIGHT 125

POWER • DRIVING FOR DISTANCE • HITTING HARD • FAIRWAY WOODS.

CHAPTER NINE 137

SLICING AND HOOKING • CAUSE AND EFFECT • CURING THE SLICE • THE MAGIC LINE • "EDUCATING" THE SLICE OR HOOK • PULLING • HOOKING • FADING AND DRAWING • SHANKING.

CHAPTER TEN 155

RECOVERY SHOTS • THE MENTAL SIDE OF BUNKERS • TECHNIQUES OUT OF SAND • OUT OF THE ROUGH • DOWNHILL AND UPHILL

LIES • AGAINST THE WIND • PUSH SHOTS • RELIEVING TENSION • FOR LEFT-HANDERS • THE INFLUENCE OF GOLF COURSE DESIGN.

CHAPTER ELEVEN   177

GOLF AS RECREATION • HOW TO PRACTICE • GETTING THAT CERTAIN FEEL • THE VALUE OF SIMPLICITY • RESOURCEFULNESS AND JUDG-MENT • SLOW PLAY • PRACTICE SWINGS • SCORING • THE IMPOR-TANCE OF PUTTING.

CHAPTER TWELVE   195

TOURNAMENT PREPARATION • COMPETITIVE ATTITUDE • CONSIS-TENCY • EIGHTEEN-HOLE MATCHES.

CHAPTER THIRTEEN   209

CONCENTRATION • COORDINATING THE SWING • GAINING EFFI-CIENCY • CONFIDENCE • STAYING ALERT • ANYTHING CAN HAPPEN.

CHAPTER FOURTEEN   227

TAKING THE BREAKS IN STRIDE • PLAYING THE WIND • DIFFICULT CONDITIONS • EQUIPMENT • GOLF ARCHITECTURE.

CHAPTER FIFTEEN   241

CONCLUSION

Foreword

By Charles Price

In the eight years preceding his retirement from formal competition at the almost laughable age of twenty-eight, Bobby Jones won 62 per cent of the national championships he entered in the two largest golfing nations there are, Great Britain and the United States. Of the thirteen titles he collected, four of them—the open and amateur championships of both these countries—were won within a single season, a feat that is known as the Grand Slam. No amateur or professional golfer before or since Jones has come close to compiling such a record, and nobody with any sense could imagine that anybody else ever will.

It would be the most natural assumption in the world to think that during those eight years Bobby Jones did little other than play golf. In reality, Jones played less formal golf during his championship years than virtually all of the players he beat, and he beat everybody in the world worth beating. Excepting the three seasons when he journeyed either to Scotland or England for Walker Cup matches and, while there, the British championships, he spent most of the tournament season playing inconsequential matches with his father and an assortment of cronies at East Lake, his home club in Atlanta, where his interests and activities ranged far beyond matters of golf. Often, he would go for months without so much as picking up a club. Instead, he studied mechanical engineering at Georgia Tech, got a degree in English literature at Harvard, dabbled in real estate, and then attended law school at Emory University. Midway through his second year, he took the state bar examinations, passed them, and so quit school to practice. As a result of these off-course activities, Jones averaged no more than three months a year playing in, and going to and from, tournaments and championships.

It would also be only natural to assume, therefore, that Jones was purely and simply a genius at golf, that he was a man who could step onto a course at any given occasion and handle a club as though it were an obedient extension of his imagination. After all, Jones was the sort of golfer who, under extreme pressure, could and did score seven 3's in a row, hole a putt of forty yards, break his own course records the day after he had set them. But he was also the sort of golfer who could come to the last three holes of a major tournament he was leading by the almost incredible margin of eighteen strokes and then limp home four over par. He could travel clear to California by train to play in an Amateur Championship he was almost certain to win and then lose in the first round to somebody the public had never heard of. He could break into tears from nervous exhaustion an hour after he had defeated the top professionals in the country. Bobby Jones was more of a human being than the headlines during his playing career would have led you to believe.

Even among sportswriters Jones had been a singular hero in a decade when they had a lot to choose from: Ruth, Grange, Dempsey, Tilden, Sande, Weismuller, Paddock, and, yes, Hagen. He had flashing good looks, a personality that could charm the blossoms off a peach tree, and the thoughtful grace of a man twice his age. (Who else might have retired at twenty-eight, having set a record so improbable that nobody then could bring it into proper perspective?) But what really set Jones apart from all the other athletes of his day, and from all the other golfers before or since him, was not so much his educated intelligence, although that had a lot to do with it, nor his modesty, although that had something to do with it, nor his native talent, although without *that* we might not be privileged to be reading this book. No, what really set him apart was his insight into the game, gorgeous in its dimensions if you have waded through the treacle and sophisms of many of the golf books which have preceded this one, the authors of which, unlike Jones, had as much to do with the actual writing of them as King James did with writing the Holy Bible. Even in his tender twenties, he was the most thoroughly intellectual golfer since Harry Vardon, the Edwardian Englishman who practically invented modern golf, and he has been matched in this respect since by perhaps only the mature Ben Hogan.

No other player so effectively reduced this fearfully complex game to such common sense. For years before Jones it had been said that if you never hit a putt as far as the distance of the hole it could not possibly drop into the hole; never up, never in. There are still some talented golfers who cannot see beyond the obviousness of the argument. But Jones did. "Of course," he said, "we never know but that the ball which is on line and stops short would have holed out. But we *do* know that the ball that ran past *did not* hole out." Hence, Jones always played his putts to "die" at the hole.

By one of the blessed accidents of golf's long, long history, Jones had to keep a meticulous diary of his thoughts on the game during the years when his native talent and his insight seemed to have been at their peaks: 1927 through 1935. During those years, he was under contract to write a column two times a week for the Bell Syndicate. Added together, these columns equaled five average novels. As editor of this book, it was mainly my job to reduce these words to the eighty-odd thousand you now have in your hands, a job that often made me feel about as necessary as a photographer for *Reader's Digest*. Almost any eighty-odd thousand words would have made a better book on golf than I have ever read before. Since all of these columns were unfailingly articulate, what I tried to save from each was the timeless. Such as:

On learning: "Golf is the one game I know which becomes more and more difficult the longer one plays it."

On windy conditions: "A headwind should be regarded as part of the golf course—just so many yards added to the hole."

On thirty-six-hole matches: "I admit that eighteen holes constitute a 'round' of golf, but since this came about by accident rather than design, the fact furnishes no reason why eighteen holes should be a 'test' of golf."

On championship pressure: "One always feels that he is running from something without knowing exactly what nor where it is."

On timing: "Nobody ever swung a golf club too slowly."

When I was through with what I thought was a masterpiece, Jones then took the manuscript and, over a period of months, picked apart every chapter, every paragraph, every sentence, every phrase of his own writing until he was sure that thirty years had not dimmed what he had truly meant to say. Well, now I know another one of the many reasons why I have never won thirteen national championships.

This is not meant to be a book to be read at one sitting— if you can help it. But however you read it, make sure you *really* read it. There is no more rewarding reading in the whole library of golf.

C.P.

Introduction

This book is composed of a number of sections which cause it to be an assortment of general readings in golf. I hope it will be useful to golfers of all classes; in helping earnest students of the game to interpret better the professional instruction they may receive, as well as to prepare them for this instruction; to aid those who would like to play better golf, but have not the time for formal instruction; to serve as a sort of reference book to which one may turn for a few minutes' reading either before or after a round. I want it to be a guide that will prove helpful before the fact, as well as a source of comfort and correction after a day when troubles have been encountered.

Most of the conversation about the improvement in the play of golf centers on the tournament players with their marvelous scoring. Even though much of this can be accounted for by better implements and better golf course conditioning, much is also due to a more widespread understanding of the fundamentals of proper technique and the willingness of intelligent young men to devote themselves to the game.

More impressive to me than this, however, is the vast number of really good players seen around country clubs and public courses. No longer, I think, does the average golfer play somewhere between 90 and 100.

So far as I know, the first effort to bring first-class players and first-class instructional methods to the public was made by A. G. Spalding about 1935 with their traveling troupe and motion picture, *Keystone of Golf*. This was followed by golf clinics held at clubs and public courses by well-known players in the employ of various manufacturing companies. The Professional Golfers Association and the United States Golf Association have for years maintained a circulating library of golf films available to clubs and other interested groups. More recently, television has brought the best players of the world to the screens of anyone interested in watching. All these must have had a lasting influence in the broad dissemination of an understanding of the swing. Even the average golfer now is a sophisticated critic.

No less than this average golfer, I have been able to keep abreast of the game and to maintain a familiarity with the methods of the top-rank players by means of the annual Masters Tournament and the television programs I have mentioned. I think I know most of the players of today about as well as I knew those with whom I played years ago. Thus I am able to claim that I have played with or observed closely every one of the outstanding players of this century, beginning with Harry Vardon and proceeding through a great number to the present-day leaders, Gary Player, Jack Nicklaus, and Arnold Palmer.

The golf swing of which I have written has been called by some the "classic" swing; but in reality there is only one sequence of movements which is entirely proper in playing a golf shot. My close observation of the game for all these years has convinced me of this fact, and I have the additional conviction that no means will be found in the future of altering the effectiveness of this sequence, that is, within the limits imposed by physical peculiarities.

It is not easy to teach golf either by personal instruction or by writing. In order to play well, the player must have the feel of the proper stroke. Being unable to view himself objectively, he has no other guide than the sensations produced by the action of his muscles. Yet the words in our language that we must use to describe feel are necessarily vague and susceptible to varying interpretations among different persons; so that no one can describe the feel of a muscular action with assurance that the description will be readily and inevitably understood by another. For this reason, I think it is necessary in all forms of golf instruction to repeat over and over descriptions of the same movements, all the while altering the modes of expression and terms of reference. Often the learner will grasp the teacher's meaning when stated in one way when he has failed to understand it in many other forms.

It is worse than useless to prescribe a rote by which the club is to be swung and the ball struck and to finish there. The pupil or prospective learner cannot possibly direct his swing through a complete sequence of correct positions as ordered by the teacher. The whole thing happens too fast to be subject to this degree of conscious control. Nevertheless, since the successful player must have a good understanding of his swing, he must be made aware of the results to be expected from all conceivable movements, right or wrong. Obviously, this procedure can result in almost endless discussions and speculations, but that is just the kind of game golf is.

To me, golf is an inexhaustible subject. I cannot imagine that anyone might ever write every word that needs to be written about the golf swing.

During the years 1927–1935, I wrote two columns each week for syndication to daily newspapers, in addition to pieces for *The American Golfer* and other publications. In 1927 O. B. Keeler and I together produced a book; in 1931 and 1932 I wrote the technical material and performed in eighteen one-reel motion pictures produced by Warner Brothers; and in 1935 I wrote the script for the motion picture mentioned before produced by Grantland Rice for A. G. Spalding. I estimate that in these activities I wrote at least a half million words about the game of golf.

The substance of these writings was drawn from my experience as a player and from my observation of many playing companions. I make no claim that my attempts at instructional writing brought anything entirely new to the literature of the game nor that they were in any sense definitive. Yet nothing in my continuing observations of the great players has caused me to alter my convictions, and it does appear significant that even today I find coming back to me in spoken words, and from the printed page, phrases I wrote more than thirty years ago. I mention this not at all as a complaint, because I am pleased to have confirmation of my views from the expert players and writers of today. The important aspect, of course, is the proof thus offered that the mechanics of the effective golfing method are generally understood today to be the same as ever. Superficial conditions may have changed somewhat, but the fundamentals remain unaltered.

The one apparently basic detail wherein the present-day professional star deviates from the classic swing described by me is in the length of the backswing for the full shot. Today the player commonly holds the club quite firmly with his left hand, never easing his grip near the top of the swing, as I did, to smooth out the change of direction from up to down. Thus the modern backswing has become shorter and the return to the ball proportionately more effortful. Forceful striking from a shorter windup is possible only because the steel shaft has made the golf club a more responsive instrument. I still think the full backswing is better for the less skillful player, because it gives him more time to build up speed before meeting the ball.

The steel shaft has yielded greater driving power, and the various wedges have helped in turning this to advantage. The sand wedge, first made truly popular by Gene Sarazen in 1932, soon caused a shot from a greenside bunker to be no more terrifying than a long approach putt, or a chip from the fringe. Soon came the pitching wedge, with which the tournament players developed a deadly accuracy. Now added driving power began to mean something when a par four of moderate length could be played with a drive and a wedge, and bunkers held no terrors.

The incentive to go all-out for length was there and the players got it. But the abbreviated windup led to a greater violence in hitting, and since much of this increased effort had to come from the legs and hips, many of our more effective players often swing themselves entirely out of the stance from which they began the stroke. These players fail to achieve the pictures of grace and poise cherished by the old-timers, but it is difficult to blame them when they are facing courses well over seven thousand yards in length.

One very selfish reason I had for publishing this book was to place between hard covers what I believe to be the more significant ideas about the playing of golf that I have expressed over the years. At the present time, these old writings are buried in newspaper morgues and other places where they are not likely ever again to see the light of day. Having managed to resurrect most of them, I decided to review these writings and to select those which I considered to be most worthy of revival.

In order to assist me in making this selection, as well as to bring to bear an unbiased and completely critical view, I was able, most happily for me, to enlist the help of Charles Price, editor of *The American Golfer* anthology and author of *The World of Golf*, in addition to many other works. Charley is not only a very skillful and prolific writer, but an experienced editor and first-rate golfer. I hope and believe that nothing without real value has escaped his paring knife. Naturally, I myself preserved as best I could the integrity of the material and have rewritten only to the extent I considered to be necessary.

The writings which formed this book represent my earnest convictions about the playing of golf during those years when my rate of performance was at its peak; that is, during the final three years of my competitive activity, followed by the three or four years when I was making motion pictures, intended to be instructional, and playing with regularity and intensity. I cannot believe that there was ever another part of my life when I thought as much about golf, or had as much incentive to seek out the right answers.

I have been happy to find that there is little in this vast amount of material that I should now care to disclaim on the basis of substance. The rewriting I have felt to be necessary has been done mainly in the hope of improving readability.

In examining and comparing the methods of various players, it is always necessary to be aware of the difference between mannerisms and fundamentals. When we set side by side the playing methods of the best golfers, we always find that the basic movements and their orderly sequence are the same within a very narrow range. What makes them all distinctive are mannerisms. I myself make the differentiation in this manner: the strict observance and accomplishment of correct fundamentals represents good form; the individualistic expression by means of mannerisms projects a player's style. So it is that no two fine golfers will present precisely the same appearance any more than will two human faces. Indeed, those golfers seen regularly are as easily recognizable by their swings as by their physical aspects.

The sophisticated student will discover in this book much that he will regard as repetitious. These repetitions are purposefully included with the thought that a slightly altered mode of expression may capture the understanding of one who has missed a similar idea expressed in another way. Such a student will also find much that is elementary. Obviously, this has been necessary because the book is intended to help players at all levels of skill. Although the top-flight player may find little that is new to him, yet I hope that even he may find some reward in an occasional perusing of this volume.

Let me repeat that I have not tried to produce a manual for instructors nor a guide for learners but rather a distillation of all that I have learned about the playing of golf during at least a half century of devotion to the game.

CHAPTER ONE

1   THE ULTIMATE OBJECT   3

2   SOME MEMORABLE ADVICE   4

3   THE FEEL OF A GOLF CLUB   5

4   HOLDING THE CLUB   5

5   MAINTAINING THE "FEEL"   9

6   THE VALUE OF GOOD FORM   11

7   SWINGING THE CLUB HEAD   13

8   HOW FORM AFFECTS SWINGING   14

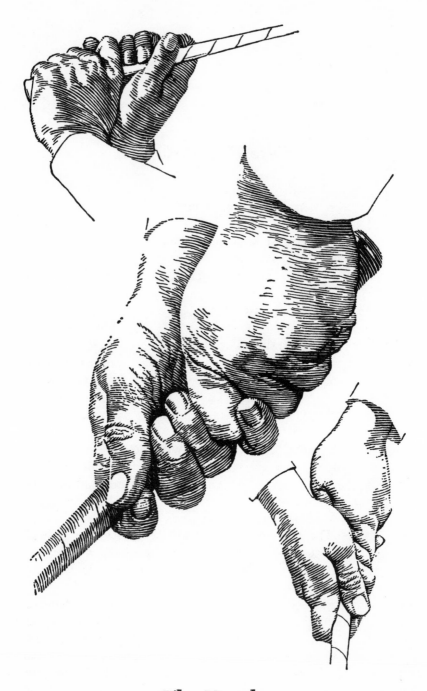

The Hands

CHAPTER ONE

I THE ULTIMATE OBJECT

With much satisfaction I often recall a shot I played at
Scioto, in Columbus, Ohio, during the last round of the
1926 National Open Championship. It was on the thirteenth hole.
I had just holed a four at the long twelfth, and had been informed
that Joe Turnesa, who was playing two holes ahead, had taken
six on that hole and five at the thirteenth. For the first time,
I began to have some hope of winning, for I was now only
two strokes behind. If I could get my four at thirteen, I should
be only a stroke behind with five holes to play.

But the thirteenth was against the wind that day, and my
spoon second, hit with every intention of bringing it in from
left to right into the wind, held straight to the line and finished
in a bunker on the left side of the green. The ball was lying
near the far bank, leaving the full width of the bunker to be
played over. The hole was a scant ten or fifteen feet beyond
the opposite bank; about six feet beyond the hole was a terrace,
which would carry the ball far away down the slope if it should
pass over the top of the rise.

In this situation, an explosive shot or blast was of no use, because
the ball, without backspin, could not be stopped short of the
downslope. It was likewise impossible to chip, because my ball
lay too far from the opposite bank of the bunker. Finally, I did
not dare to try cutting the ball up with lots of backspin, because
the lie was not good, and if I took too much sand I should
leave it still in the bunker.

I do not know what I should have or could have done had

not the bank of the bunker been low and not too precipitous. As it was, it was only a little over two feet high, and sloping. My only chance lay in a running shot, hoping to take the bank with the proper speed. I hit the ball with a four-iron, scuttling it across the sand, and watched it climb the bank. Luckily, it curled down the slope and came to rest four feet to the left of the hole. I got the next one in, and felt vastly relieved.

The general tendency, I think, is to overlook the possibilities in a shot of this nature. I admit that it does appear unworkmanlike and amateurish to run a shot through sand and out of a bunker, but it sometimes becomes necessary to disregard appearances. A few disasters resulting from a desire to display brilliant technique are enough to harden even the most sensitive nature. To approach the hole remains the ultimate object in the game. Once the round is under way, the business in hand becomes that of getting results. Nothing else matters.

2   SOME MEMORABLE ADVICE

Two of the greatest golfers of earlier times were the English professionals Harry Vardon and J. H. Taylor who, between them, won eleven British Open Championships. Among the many wise things both observed about the game, two especially impressed me. "No matter what happens," Vardon once said, "keep on hitting the ball." In effect, this is what I remembered and tried to do when playing a tournament round. Vardon was a man of immense gifts, not the least of which was his practicality.

J. H. Taylor made the statement that all the great golfers he had known had possessed a quality he chose to call "courageous timidity." That happy phrase expresses exactly the qualities a golfer, expert or not, must have in order to get the most from whatever mechanical ability he may have. He must have courage to keep trying in the face of ill luck or disappointment, and timidity to appreciate and appraise the dangers of each stroke, and to curb the desire to take chances beyond reasonable hope of success. There can be no doubt that such a combination in itself embraces and makes possible all the other qualities—determination, concentration, nerve—we acclaim as parts of the ideal golfing temperament for the championship contender as well as for the average golfer.

3   THE FEEL OF A GOLF CLUB

There is nothing occult about hitting a golf ball. In fact, although the application may be a bit more complicated, we use no more than the ordinary principles of motion we encounter numberless times every day. Once started upon a correct path, the club will tend to hold to its course until outside forces cause a change.

The great fault in the average golfer's conception of his stroke is that he considers the shaft of the club a means of transmitting actual physical force to the ball, whereas it is in reality merely the means of imparting velocity to the club head. We would all do better could we only realize that the length of a drive depends not upon the brute force applied but upon the speed of the club head. It is a matter of velocity rather than of physical effort of the kind that bends crowbars and lifts heavy weights.

I like to think of a golf club as a weight attached to my hands by an imponderable medium, to which a string is a close approximation, and I like to feel that I am throwing it at the ball with much the same motion I should use in cracking a whip. By the simile, I mean to convey the idea of a supple and lightning-quick action of the wrists in striking—a sort of flailing action.

4   HOLDING THE CLUB

The huntsman knows that to cant the gun is one of the worst things he can do. So the golfer ought to know that in order to achieve success he must maintain a fixed relation throughout the swing between his hands and the face of his club. Yet many times, striving for complete relaxation, he takes such a loose grip upon the club that the least disturbing motion will cause it to turn in his hands. Many times, too, I have seen a really good player spoil a shot by loosening too much the grip of the left hand at the top of the swing. When addressing the ball, the player places his hands upon the club in a definite position, and in that position they must remain.

A strained grip upon the club tenses the muscles in the forearms and tends to stiffen members that ought to be supple and active during the stroke; but the grip may be firm without introducing the least bit of rigidity in any part of the body.

In my conception of the stroke, it is always the left arm that should be the guiding member. In the case of nearly all good players, it is the left arm that starts and controls the direction of the stroke until it comes time to hit.

For this reason, a firm grip of the left hand is the proper means of maintaining the relation between hands and club head. As the left arm remains practically straight throughout the backswing, any tightening of the forearm and wrists caused by the firmer grip will cause less damage there than in the right arm, which on the way back should be relaxed and following easily as the left directs. The right wrist and arm are the primary means of supplying speed and imparting force culminating at the ball. They should therefore remain relaxed throughout the stroke. Let us simply say that the left arm must keep the swing on track; the right hand must be responsible for timing and touch.

Those who reverse this order, maintaining a firm grip with the right hand, a flabby hold with the left—and this is not at all uncommon among beginners who are accustomed to playing right-handed games—these will lift the club to the shoulder instead of swinging it back. None will obtain a sufficient turn of the hips and shoulders, and the position at the top of the swing, with both arms bent, will be wholly lacking in poise. The impression is that such a player, if he hits the ball at all, will do so only because of the kindness of fortune.

The average golfer is ever conscious of walking a narrow path, afraid of tumbling off on one side or the other. He is caught between the danger of losing the effect of the wrist-cock if he holds

firmly to the club and that of an insecure grip if he relaxes enough
to allow a sufficient flexibility in his wrists. He must find a middle
ground of safety.

The place for him to look is the grip of his left hand upon
the club. Obviously, the shaft must not turn in his hands while
he is making his stroke. So his grip must be positive and firm;
and quite as obviously, if the left wrist is to be cocked, his grip
must not produce any degree of stiffness in the wrist joint.

The grip of the left hand should be arranged so that the
shaft of the club lies diagonally across the palm but is held mainly
by the fingers. At the position of address, the club should rest
upon the middle joint of the index finger of the left hand, but
the most positive part of the grip of this hand should be exerted
by the two smaller fingers and the middle finger.

Holding the club in this way allows a certain amount of relaxation in forearm and wrist without disturbing the security of
the grip. If the club were held to any extent in the palm of
the hand, exerting the pressure necessary to keep it from turning
would freeze or solidify the wrist joint and render ample cocking impossible. But held by the fingers, the hand need not be
clenched, but may even be opened slightly to assist the cocking,
without disturbing the grip.

It is important that the effort to complete a full backswing
should not disturb the left thumb. It is not uncommon to find
a player who allows this thumb to slide down the shaft as the
length of his backswing produces a strain in his faulty grip.
Especially is this likely to occur when the thumb is placed directly
on top of the shaft at address. A thumb directly on top at the
beginning is found directly underneath at the top; and thus sub-
jected to severe strain. Placing it a little upon the side eases this
strain and still leaves it where it can prevent the shaft from slipping into the V between the thumb and index finger.

In the end the problem here, as in every other detail of the
golf stroke, is to maintain a perfect balance between firmness
and relaxation in the interests of control and rhythm.

In considering golfing tips and their worth, or rather lack of
worth, one cannot help thinking of the favorite quick cure for
a hook or slice involving the shifting of the position of the right
hand upon the club; the right hand more under the shaft to cor-

rect a slice, and more over to correct a hook. It is familiar music, of course, but if there ever was a pure tip, having no relation to the promulgation of sound golfing information, this is it.

A correct grip is a fundamental necessity in the golf swing. It might even be said to be the first necessity, for a person must take hold of the club before he can swing it, and he must hold it correctly before it becomes physically possible for him to swing it correctly. But there was never a more pernicious thought than that the grip is something to go tinkering with in order to counteract some mistake made in swinging. Few average golfers or duffers grip the club correctly. Most should alter the position of one hand or the other, or of both, but the change should be permanent and not merely as a temporary corrective.

I began playing golf at the age of six, with the interlocking grip. I played in this way for about two years, and then changed to the overlapping. So far as I know, my grip was from then on precisely as it was when I was eight years old, or nine, whenever it was I made this change. Since that time, I experimented with changes, in order to correct temporary faults, just enough to know that they do more harm than good.

In the correct grip, the two hands should be able to function as nearly as possible as one, and their placement should encourage easy handling of the club throughout the swing. If a player is not in the habit of employing a grip that fills this bill, he should immediately alter it until it does; but after altering his grip until it is correct and comfortable, let him resolve never to change it. If something goes wrong, let him look elsewhere for the trouble, for the hands form the connection with the club; through the hands the player is able to sense the location and alignment of the club; they are the keys to his control; the slightest change leaves him groping.

The worst mistake possible in gripping the club is to separate the actions of the two hands. It is not necessary to distinguish between the overlapping, interlocking, and old-fashioned grips. Any one is good enough if the hands are placed so they can work together.

Some little latitude is allowable, but it is very small. The left hand must be in a position of power—it must be placed so that it can swing the club through without jamming the left elbow against the side. It must, therefore, be well up on top of the shaft. The beginner who holds his club so that he can see the tips of the fingers of his left hand is hopeless until he changes.

Similarly, the right hand must not be placed too far under the shaft because from this position, it may turn over in the act of hitting. If the left hand has been placed correctly, it is not likely that the right will be placed too much on top, for this would require a contortion no one is likely to endure in order to cause himself trouble.

The correct grip can be demonstrated more easily than it can be described. I should recommend to any player who is not absolutely sure that he is right, that he check his grip immediately with a competent instructor. Until he is right here, he is not ready for anything else.

One more thing should always be remembered. It is the complaint of all golfers that on some days they have the feel and on others the magic touch entirely deserts them. Many times I have found that by shifting my grip up or down upon certain clubs, particularly the driver and putter, I have been able to bring back the touch with these clubs. Often the slightly altered balance of the club, making it feel lighter or heavier as the grip is shifted down or up, is all that is needed to restore confidence.

5 MAINTAINING THE "FEEL"

"Why is it," someone asks, "that a fairly good golfer—that is, one who can play close to 80 on occasions—can sometimes possess what we call the "feel" to such a degree that he can hit the ball really well, and then can suddenly lose all sense of hitting until he can't play at all? Is it because he can't play while he is thinking about his swing?"

It seems to me that this question implies that the better player, or expert, is able to play golf without thinking of anything at all except where he wants the ball to go. I know a good many fine young chaps engaged in big-time competition who would be highly pleased if this were so.

Unquestionably, there are times when first-class players can play the game subconsciously. But the average player should remember that the most accomplished golfer can lose the touch as suddenly and for as little apparent reason as anyone else, and that, although at times he can immediately discover and correct his fault, there are also times when he is entirely at a loss for a remedy.

This does not mean that the expert does not know how he should swing the club. But golf is a difficult game to play consistently well because the correct swing is not a thing the human body can accomplish entirely naturally. To hit the ball correctly, the golfer has always to be under restraint. I have always, in my own mind, likened this restraint to that under which a trotting or a pacing horse must labor in a race when he must hold to an artificial gait although every urge must be for him to run like blazes.

So any golfer may for a while have the feel so that he may think he can go on playing in that way easily and naturally; but the trouble is that the moment some mental impulse or physical necessity suggests to one of his muscles that it do something else at a particular time, it is likely to yield, because the thing it is doing is not the thing it can do most easily. A golfer who depends upon finding the feel more or less accidentally can never hope to play consistently well, day in and out, for this very reason. He must know how to hit a golf ball and he must know when and where in his swing to apply the restraint I have mentioned.

The answer to the question that started all this is, "Not because he can't play while he is thinking of the swing, but because he isn't sure what he ought to think about, and what he ought to try to do." Granted, of course, that there could be those who have an irreproachable conception of the golf stroke, yet have not enough muscular control or sense of timing to play well; still that does not alter the proposition that the man who has the muscular control and sense of timing cannot play consistently well unless he knows what he is doing.

But I think the nature of the problem is indicated when we realize that even the man with the control, the sense, and the knowledge finds intervals when his game is off and he can't find the reason. There are so many places to look and so many checks to make—and sometimes the trouble is found in the simplest and least obvious locations. Golf is a game that must always be uncertain. I don't believe that anyone will ever master it to the extent that several have mastered billiards and chess. If someone should do so, I think he would give it up—but that is a danger most of us would be willing to risk.

6 THE VALUE OF GOOD FORM

I am sure that the average golfer, trying to absorb and use the mass of instructive material given to him, wishes at times that it could all be reduced to a very few points that he might readily grasp and apply. The person concerned with helping him wishes, too, that this might be possible; but little things—often very little things—matter a great deal in golf. When one thinks that even a trained eye will have difficulty detecting the difference between the swing that produces a perfect shot and that which results in a foozle, the importance of small variations can be better appreciated. The perfection of timing and the precision of striking required to produce a perfect golf shot allow as little leeway as anything in sport.

Obviously, even all golfers of the first rank do not swing their clubs in exactly the same way; but it is rare, indeed, that one finds a successful player who violates or omits any of the recognized fundamentals of the correct swing. It is always possible to make some amount of correction or compensation while the swing is under way, so that a superior sense of control may enable one individual to get away with things another could not risk. I have a friend who insists that his only good shots result when he makes the same number of mistakes coming down that he made going up.

But to the person who is trying to develop a reasonably sound swing, corrective or compensatory movements should be of little interest. Good form simplifies the action until each essential move-

ment flows into each succeeding essential, and complications requiring timing and correction are reduced to a minimum. The
unorthodox swinger may on a particular day, when he is "right,"
outplay the man of sound method, but over the long run the
latter will certainly hold an advantage.

Obviously the sound swing is not a definite reality. We all
recognize that no two players swing the club in exactly the same
manner, yet certainly more than one deserves to be regarded as a
sound swinger. The trained observer and student of the game,
over a long period of close observance and intimate contact with
successful players, in time fixes upon several actions and postures
that are common to all. He learns to separate the mannerisms of
the individual from the basic elements of the swing, and gradually builds up a conception of a correct set of motions which he
regards as essential in playing the game expertly. When he says
that a certain swing is sound, he means that regardless of variations
peculiar to the individual, the method still embraces and accounts
for all correct actions and postures or enough of them to assure
a high rate of success.

The first requisite of a truly sound swing is simplicity. In this
respect, I think that the late Horton Smith and Lady Heathcoat-
Amory, who as Miss Joyce Wethered played superb golf in my
day, excel any golfers I have ever seen. Each reduced the matter
of hitting the ball to two motions: with one, the club was taken
back; with the other, it was swung through. I have found many
to agree with me that Miss Wethered's swing was the most perfect in the world, but I think it is safe to say that Horton Smith's
backswing was the simplest. Either of these makes an ideal model
to be imitated by anyone, for in these two methods it was possible
to see all the fundamentals without the confusing effect of mannerisms.

It will be found also that the sound swing is very graceful.
This does not mean that any graceful motion is necessarily sound,
but one cannot execute the various motions, nor assume successively the correct postures, in rhythmic style, without effecting a
pleasing appearance. The sound swing flows from beginning to
end, but it flows powerfully, and is graceful because it is correct,
rather than because it is made so. To me, the performance of the

perfect golf stroke is as much a thing of beauty as can be found in any of the performing arts.

The simple swing that is also sound will be susceptible to repetition through a number of performances. This is the basis of consistency on the golf course.

7 SWINGING THE CLUB HEAD

Two of golf's most eminent instructors, Macdonald Smith and Ernest Jones, built all their teaching around the one conception, "Swing the club head." There are other details to be thought of, of course, in developing anything like a sound swing, but in the end it will be found that this is the prime necessity. Those who are able to sense what it means to "swing the club head" will find that they can thus cover up a multitude of sins, and those who sense it not will find that no amount of striving for perfection in positioning will quite take its place.

In order to make easier the discovery of this sense of swinging, the club must be swung back far enough so that there will be no need for hurry or quickened effort coming down. This is the one point I have tried to stress more than anything else— the necessity for an ample backswing if one is truly to swing the club head. The man who allows himself only a short backswing can never be a swinger, because his abbreviated length does not allow space for a smooth acceleration to get him up to speed by the time the club reaches the ball.

Rhythm and timing we all must have, yet no one knows how to teach either. The nearest approach to an appreciation of what they are is in this conception of swinging. The man who hits at the ball, rather than through it, has no sense of rhythm; similarly, the man who, after a short backswing, attempts to make up for lost space by a convulsive effort initiating the downstroke has no sense of rhythm.

The only one who has a chance to achieve a rhythmic, well-timed stroke is the man who, in spite of all else, yet swings his club head, and the crucial area is where the swing changes direction at the top. If the backswing can be made to flow back leisurely, and to an ample length, from where the start downward can be made without the feeling that there may not be enough time left, there is good chance of success. But a hurried backswing induces a hurried start downward, and a short backswing makes some sort of rescue measures imperative. A good golfer will not like to be guilty of either.

Two of the important points in the swinging machinery are the wrists and hips; if the wrists do not flex easily, or if the trunk does not turn readily, a true swing cannot be accomplished. Stiff or wooden wrists shorten the backswing and otherwise destroy the feel of the club head. Without the supple connection of relaxed and active wrist joints, and a delicate, sensitive grip, the golf club, which has been so carefully weighted and balanced, might just as well be a broom handle with nothing on the end. The club head cannot be swung unless it can be felt on the end of the shaft.

So swing, swing, swing, if you want to play better golf; fight down any tautness wherever it may make its appearance; strive for relaxed muscles throughout, and encourage a feeling of laziness in the backswing and the start downward. Go back far enough, trust your swing, and then—swing the club head through.

8   HOW FORM AFFECTS SWINGING

The man with a faulty swing ties himself up so that a smooth stroke becomes impossible. The expert swings smoothly because his successive positions are easy and comfortable, and are such that the movement from one to the other is not hampered by unwilling muscles. The average golfer does not swing smoothly because at some stage he creates a condition that makes it easier for him to move in the wrong direction than in the right one.

Here is an example of how one faulty position or movement can upset a swing, when, with this one fault corrected, it is able to function reasonably well. The swing, being my own, is one with which I can claim to be fairly familiar; and, when the trouble appeared, it marked the first time in at least ten years when I had developed a fault I could not detect and work out for myself within a reasonable time.

For several months, the old feeling of comfort and smoothness had entirely escaped me, especially with the woods—the irons had not been so bad. I noted that my swing was abnormally fast, and particularly that my legs were not working just right. I tried everything that had worked in the past—slowing down, exaggerating the forward shift of my hips at the start of the downstroke, watching the wrist-cock to make certain of getting the left side into the stroke—but still I could not bring back the accustomed rhythm. I did suspect that the trouble was in my feet, for I could not be even nearly comfortable in the stance and address position, which upon examination appeared to be as usual.

So, despairing of ever working the thing out myself, I took out George Sargent, who was then professional at my home club, to knock around a few holes and talk the thing over. At first, of course, he could only see that my swing did not look as it used to look, that the rhythm was gone, and that it lacked power. Searching back from effect to cause, after we had played five holes, he happened to be standing directly behind my back as I hit a brassie shot. Immediately he caught it. In addressing the ball, my right heel was entirely off the ground.

Now, let's see what the effect of this could be. My right knee was bent abnormally and what weight rested on the right foot was supported on the toe. Obviously, this made a normal stance, with both feet about on line, very uncomfortable. With only the toe of this foot supporting the weight, I had to draw the right foot well back to maintain any sort of balance. But the worst part of it was that the precarious balance made a smooth start back impossible. There was an irresistible impulse to get back to earth quickly, and my backswing always started with a jerk. Straightening the right leg a bit—it should never be perfectly straight or rigid at the beginning—and lowering the right heel to the ground made my balance secure again, and I was able to start back without hurry.

The two danger points are at the start of the backswing and at the start of the downstroke. To start back smoothly avoids haste later on; to start down in leisurely fashion helps to maintain the perfect balance, and provides for well-timed, accurate striking.

CHAPTER TWO

1   EASE AND COMFORT   19

2   SHIFTING THE WEIGHT   21

3   PLACING THE FEET   22

4   PROPER POSTURE   26

5   POSITIONING THE BALL   27

6   THE PROCEDURE IN ADDRESSING THE BALL   28

7   VARIATIONS IN THE STANCES   29

8   STAYING IN MOTION   30

9   THE POSITION OF THE HEAD   32

10 "REACHING" FOR THE BALL   34

11 AN INSIDIOUS HABIT   35

The Address

CHAPTER TWO

I EASE AND COMFORT

One day when my father and I were playing together, he was driving last from the back of a very long tee. With a swing that could only be described as labored, he bashed the head of his driver into the turf so that the ball popped almost straight up, and dropped just in front of the teeing ground. As we started forward, he called to me, "Come back here a minute." Then, with as graceful a swing as I could imagine, he clipped a dandelion from the grass. Glaring at me, he said in a strangely challenging tone, "Now what's the matter with that swing?" "Nothing," I said, "why don't you use it sometime?"

There is not one golfer in the world who has not at some time thought how fine it would be if he could swing at the ball as freely and as smoothly as he swings at a clover top or a piece of paper lying on the grass. Some, indeed, do not even then have to others the graceful and effective appearance they conceive themselves to have, but there is no denying, except in the case of experts, that the practice swing is, almost always, far better than that made with the intent of striking the ball. The player himself senses and admits this difference, often recognizes the reason, yet fails to understand that there is a sensible way to overcome it.

Most persons accept it as one of those things that must be suffered. The necessity for the existence of this difference is lamented, accepted, and we pass on. The entire business is attributed to a mental condition, a sense of responsibility, anxiety, fear, or whatnot, setting up a tension that cannot be overcome. This much is true, but it so happens that it is only a part of the story. The difference in the state of mind of the player when taking a practice swing and when playing an actual stroke is easily understood and its effect appreciated; but what is neither understood nor appreciated is that the elimination or omission of some of the frills of the actual stroke that are not present in the practice swing may work a complete change. The expert is not afraid of the ball, because he has learned to have confidence in his ability to hit it.

Watch a moderately good average golfer take a practice swing preparatory to making a shot. He swings the club easily, rhythmically to and fro, there is a proper balance throughout and a commendable relaxation. The stance is always conservative and comfortable—one into which he has stepped naturally without fuss or bother. Now watch him as he steps up to the ball. He first sets his feet wide apart—at least farther apart than they were before. This, he thinks, is to assure good balance and a firm footing.

Then he begins to waggle, and the more he waggles the more he bends over the ball and the more tense he becomes. Instead of sensing the correct position, or of falling naturally into a comfortable one, he attempts to set himself before the ball with perfect accuracy, attempting to see that everything is placed just so.

I have no quarrel with anyone for taking pains with a shot nor for making certain that he is ready to play before he starts the swing. But most golfers lose sight of the fact that in the first position it is ease and comfort that are to be sought, and that a strained or unnatural posture was never recommended by anyone.

The general criticisms of the average player's posture at address are that his feet are too far apart, his body is bent too much, and his arms are extended too far. These are the most common faults, and every one of them is unnatural. The natural way to stand is with the feet separated, but not set wide apart; the natural bend of the body is very slight, with the weight more back on the heels and never entirely on the toes; and the natural disposition of the arms is to allow them to hang almost straight down from the shoulders.

It is very rare that tension is observed in a practice swing, and this is so because the player, not feeling the necessity of being entirely correct, comes closer to assuming a natural posture. Let him take this naturalness into the actual shot; let him simplify his preliminary motions as much as possible; and let him start the ball on its way without hurry, yet without setting himself on point before it like a fine bird dog on a covey of quail. In this way, he can go a long way, on the physical side, toward overcoming the understandable mental disturbances that must arise when he is confronted by the responsibility of hitting the ball. Mental tension—that is, keenness—never does any harm when it is accompanied by physical relaxation.

2 SHIFTING THE WEIGHT

How many times have you seen a left foot fly up in the air as its owner struck at a golf ball? I believe you would like to have a new ball for every one you have seen. I would not be surprised if you have noticed this movement to be characteristic of the swings of a good many of your acquaintances, for it is one of the commonest of all golfing faults.

I have said that waving the left foot is a fault. It is really an evidence, or result, of a fault. The real fault is in the falling back, in shifting the weight or permitting it to shift backward during the hitting stroke—and there is nothing worse in golf—except, possibly, hitting the ball with the wrong end of the club.

There are at least three things that can cause a man to be guilty of this mistake. First, he may address the ball with too much weight on his left foot and keep it there during the backswing; second, he may start right but shift to his left foot going back; and, third, he may not shift incorrectly, but start from a position so far ahead of the ball that he will have to move backward in order to hit it. In any case, he finds that he is trying to hit the ball while falling away from it—attempting to move his hands and club in one direction while his weight and the great power of his body are moving in another—a thing so preposterous that it is not really worthwhile saying that it is bad.

I do not believe that it is necessary to shift the weight backward during the backswing; certainly, I know it is not if the player stands sufficiently behind the ball when he is addressing it. If he insists upon addressing the ball off his right foot, then he may set himself right by means of this backward shift. But he must get his weight behind the stroke if he is going to hit the ball correctly.

Hitting a golf ball is like hitting anything else in that it cannot be hit hard or efficiently if it is behind the striker. He cannot reach back to get it without sacrificing a world of power. When a good swing starts down, everything ought to move together toward the ball. The left heel should come down, the hips should shift forward, the arms and clubhead should move with the rest. If there is one single part of the mechanism moving in another direction, setting up a counterforce and partially overcoming the force directed toward the ball, then the stroke will be inefficient, less powerful than it ought to be.

This should not be hard to understand. No one would attempt to throw a baseball while reared back on his heels or to deliver a right uppercut while stepping away from his foe. Why, then, should he fling his left foot at the water bucket when he tries to hit a golf ball?

3   PLACING THE FEET

The average golfer, when he is going out for length to add those few additional yards to his normal drive, cannot resist an impulse to spread his feet just a bit farther apart. It is natural, of course, to feel that a firmer, more fixed stance is necessary in order to brace himself against the effect of the extra exertion and, in order to make sure that the footing is solid, the ambitious one

will invariably work his feet into the ground as though he were
getting set to lift a piano. He thinks he is getting set to hit harder,
but he is in reality beating himself at the start.

The most tremendous span in a golf stance was that accomplished by Major Charles O. Hezlet, the British Walker Cup
player. Once while playing with the Major I made an attempt
to take the exact stance he had employed for a drive. By great
effort, I could make my legs cover the distance, but once in the
position, I had no earthly chance of hitting a golf shot. Certainly,
if a wide stance were an aid in getting distance, Major Hezlet
would have been an astonishingly long driver. He was about as
firmly fixed to the earth as one could possibly be, yet while he
was a very straight driver and a fine player, he was far from
being an exceptionally long hitter. His forte was, rather, his
ability with his short, almost pivotless swing to hit the ball time
and time again down the middle of the fairway. Major Hezlet
elected to employ a wide stance because for him the advantage
gained by improved control more than offset the length he was
thus forced to sacrifice.

There are several sources of power in the ordinary golf stroke.
The arms, wrists, shoulders, and hips all contribute toward the
aggregate force that should be exploded exactly behind the ball.
The ideal, of course, is a proper balance among all these factors
that will allow each to contribute as much power as possible
without disturbing the accuracy of the stroke. Anything causing
a loss or an impairment of the efficiency of any one of these
factors will cause a loss of power in the entire stroke.

A stance as extreme as Major Hezlet's practically destroys the
value of hip turn as a contributor to distance. With the feet spread
wide apart, the lower part of the body is almost completely
locked, and even the shoulder motion is made more difficult. The
result is brought about, though in lesser degree, by any increase
the player may take over his normal span.

The keynote of the address position should be ease, comfort,
and relaxation. Above all else, the first posture must be one from
which the movement of the swing may start smoothly without
having to break down successive barriers of tension set up by
taut or strained muscles. To go a bit further, the player should

feel himself alert, sensitive to impulses, and ready to move in either direction.

It is always better at this point to be one's own natural self than to try to look like someone else. Any posture that feels uncomfortable is certain to produce a strain somewhere that will cause the ensuing movement to be jerky. It is well to remember that there are no forces outside the player's own body that have to be resisted or balanced. There is no need for him to set or brace himself, for there is nothing to brace against. If one could conceive that he were standing naturally, with a club in his hands, engaged in ordinary conversation, and that he then bent over enough to ground the club behind a ball not too far away, the resulting posture would be quite good.

This position, where everything is more or less at rest, is the most easily observed of the entire stroke, and it is the first to which the beginner should give attention. It is difficult to swing the club correctly, but it ought not to be a hard job to assume a correct position from which to start.

Taking first the stance, the position of the feet is all we have to consider. At first, I think the player should give himself little concern about the placing of his feet with respect to the ball, disregarding this feature to the extent of learning the correct stance before attempting to address the ball. The most important thing about the feet is to place them in such positions that they will not hinder the motion of the body during any part of the stroke. This must be done whether the stance be open, closed, or square, and whether the player finds himself more comfortable with his feet close together or far apart.

The best pros, almost without exception, place the right foot so that the toe points almost exactly straight to the front, at right angles to the line of play. Never in select golfing company do we see a right toe pointing more than ever so slightly outward away from the ball. The left toe, on the other hand, usually is turned slightly outward, away from the ball, and never inward toward the ball.

This is the correct position because it is the position from which the complete swing may be most easily accomplished. With the right foot pointing almost straight ahead, a turn of the hips causes the right knee to swing back and form a splendid brace, as it must. If the foot were turned either way, it would interfere with the stroke either going up or coming down, simply because the motion of the leg could not conform with the hip turn if the foot were far from the proper place. Turning the right toe outward destroys the right-leg brace, and interferes with a free swing through the ball; turning the left toe outward prevents a full backswing by restricting the action of the left leg.

When one stands naturally erect, with feet approximately twelve inches apart and each in a natural position as in walking, there is a perfect balance of the body, and a complete facility of movement in either direction without destroying that balance. Hips and shoulders can be twisted and turned, arms swung, and the entire torso turned to either side with equal ease. This is what we are striving for in addressing a golf ball, and the positions of the feet have a great deal to do with the value of the position. The more like a natural standing posture the thing can be made, the better off we are.

The exact location of the ball with respect to the feet is not a matter of first importance so long as certain considerations are not lost sight of. The first of these is that a preponderance of weight must not be upon the right foot. There should be an approximately equal division of the burden, but if either foot is to carry more, it should by all means be the left foot. Regardless of what is said by those who like to talk about swaying, it is necessary in order to swing easily and rhythmically that there be an appreciable shift of weight successively backward to the right foot in taking the club back and forward to the left in striking the ball. This cannot be done if too much weight rests upon the right foot at the start.

The most usual position of the ball is on a spot opposite the left heel of the player, or perhaps a very few inches back of that point. There is an important requirement of good form that limits the advance of the ball beyond the left foot, just as the requirement of weight distribution makes it necessary to keep the ball ahead of the right foot.

It will be noted that the better players uniformly address the ball so that the hands of the player are ahead of the ball and the shaft of the club inclines backward to the head, resting behind the ball. This is a very important feature, because the position of the hands assists materially in keeping the club face open. The left hand, being the factor that opens or closes the face, should be placed on the club with the back of the hand upward. This position can only be maintained if the hands are advanced beyond the spot opposite the ball, so that the club will slant backward to its position on the ground.

4   PROPER POSTURE

There is one point that ought to be noticed in which the better players are alike and the dubs are uniformly out of step. That point has solely to do with the degree of rigidity to be found in the knee joints. Many beginners, for some reason, stiffen one or both legs to the point where all spring and mobility is taken away. The knee joints are thrown backward and locked so that the legs become like pieces of wood. Watching any good player closely, it will be observed that each leg is relaxed and supple—not bent into a squatting posture, but far from the rigid straightness of the dub. The desired curvature is about that accomplished in walking leisurely at a comfortable speed.

The man who reaches out for the ball gets into trouble because he cannot extend his arms and remain relaxed. The extreme of this is often seen in the player who extends his arms and elevates his hands until arms, hands, and club complete a straight line from his shoulders to the ball. The teaching that the left arm and the club should lie in the same vertical plane is all right, but no one in his wildest moments ever conceived that they should lie in the same plane in any other direction.

I always like to see a person stand up to a golf ball as though he were perfectly at home in its presence, in a posture that appears easy and comfortable from top to bottom. To accomplish this, it is only necessary to stand erect, with feet just far enough

apart to accommodate a little footwork when the body is turned
from side to side; then to bend over slightly, just enough to assure
that when the arms hang naturally downward, the hands will have
free passage across the front of the body.

5   POSITIONING THE BALL

It seems to me that one of the most important things for the
golfer to watch is the matter of keeping his weight behind
the ball. For some reason, it is difficult for the player himself
to be aware of the exact location of the ball with respect to his
feet. The almost universal tendency is to creep more and more
ahead until the player suddenly finds that at address the ball is
directly opposite his right foot, when he would have sworn it
was opposite his left.

In order to strike a blow at any object with the full power of
which a particular human mechanism is capable, the force of the
blow must be contributed to by every muscle and by every ounce
of power in that mechanism. Any force or any portions of weight
moving in a direction counter to the direction of the blow must
inevitably take away some of the sting.

This is what usually occurs when a golfer allows himself to
get in front of the ball. Very soon he finds that he must reach
backward in order to strike it. He finds that if his weight is
permitted to go forward into the shot as it normally would, a
badly smothered hook will result, and, in order to avoid this,
he will begin to hold his weight back on the right foot or shift
it backward even more. This is when slicing or topping begins.

With the ball placed well forward—that is, about on line with
the instep of the left foot—at the top of the swing one will have
the feeling that he can throw the whole weight and power of his
body into the stroke, with the further advantage that the advanced position of the ball gives him more time to swing the club
head into proper alignment. With the ball placed farther back, the

tendency is to abbreviate the backswing and to yank the club down from the top before the player has swung himself into a hitting position.

The average player also has trouble moving the left hip out of the way of the stroke in time to allow a free passage for the arms. This will make more trouble if he starts his swing standing to any degree in front of the ball, for subconsciously he will hesitate to move his body to any extent for fear he will place himself in a position from which he cannot hit. If the ball is placed farther forward, a free turn and flowing swing will be encouraged.

6   THE PROCEDURE IN ADDRESSING THE BALL

The close observer will note that almost all first-class players take their stances in substantially the same way. The procedure is about like this: the player will walk up to the ball from behind, all the while looking toward the objective and planning the shot he is about to play; as he nears the ball, he will ground his club behind it; then, still aware of his objective, he will place his left foot so as to provide proper alignment; now he need only drop the right foot back into a comfortable position and take as many waggles as he likes (in my case, this was usually one) before starting the backswing.

This procedure accomplishes several things. First, it fixes the distance from the feet to the ball in the best of all ways by accommodating the distance to the comfortable extent of the arms and club. I cannot imagine taking my stance without first having some measure of this distance. The second advantage is that the player has approached the ball in the normal relaxed posture of ordinary walking; and approaching the ball from behind, he may stop where his body will be behind the stroke and he may set himself naturally, with his weight properly distributed.

7   VARIATIONS IN THE STANCES

I remember one night at the Marine Hotel in Gullane, Scotland, back in 1926, when the British Amateur was being played at Muirfield, George Duncan, the sporadically brilliant British professional, was expounding to a few of us his latest theory of the golf swing. George expressed the belief that the most important part of the business was accomplished by the knees and feet. He described and illustrated for us how he was "playing golf with his feet"; the "takeoff" from the left foot originating the motion of the backswing.

Without either subscribing to or denying the correctness of Duncan's ideas—indeed, I think they might be helpful to some as well as ruinous for others—it is safe to say that a great many players allow their feet to spoil too many shots. It is too easy to set down one foot in such a position that it will embarrass the stroke without being aware of the mistake until the swing has gotten under way, which is, of course, too late. A little more care in intelligently cultivating the habit of proper placing will be well rewarded.

It is a fine thing for the golfer always to remember what he can do with his feet. Many times a tendency to hook or slice can be corrected by a small adjustment of the stance; or if the player has advanced far enough to attempt such things, he can in the same way bring off a draw or a fade at will. It is not so much that the altered positions directly affect the stroke, but that variations are induced when the player places himself in postures most encouraging to them.

The closed stance is regarded as the hooking stance, and the open stance as the more likely to produce a fade or slice. The reasons are obvious. To assume a closed stance position, the player pulls his right foot back away from the ball so that it rests several inches behind a line through his left foot parallel to the line of flight. This accomplishes two things: first, it encourages a round, flat swing with a free turn away from the ball; and, second, it sets up a certain amount of resistance in the left side at about the time of impact. Addressing the ball in this manner encourages the player to hit outward at the ball, and when he exaggerates the maneuver, he may have the feeling of taking the ball upon the club face and swinging it around to the left.

When this results in a wide, sweeping hook, I have known some of my Scottish professional friends to call this "a Scot's shot—he held onto it too long."

The open stance, on the other hand, is not a position of power, but rather of control. With the right foot advanced, the player stands more directly over the ball and has more difficulty in turning his hips and shoulders during the backstroke. From this position, he cannot easily accomplish a flat swing; hence, he is apt to be more upright. The open-stance advocate will be more likely to slice than to hook and will likely play most of his iron shots with a slight left to right drift. In the open position, the player faces more toward the hole. Even at address, his left hip is moved backward out of the way of the passage of his hands; at the same time, the right side is advanced so that it becomes an impediment to a round, sweeping swing. These two factors encourage cutting across the ball, which is a characteristic of players who use this stance.

8 STAYING IN MOTION

The function of the waggle and the movement of the body preceding the actual beginning of the backswing is to avoid or destroy tension in the position from which the swing is to make its start. Smoothness is an essential quality of the correct golf stroke, and since a smooth start cannot be made if the muscles are tense or the posture strained, it is of the utmost importance that the player should be completely relaxed and comfortable as he addresses the ball. Provided the waggle and the player's manner of falling into his first position accomplish this, it matters little what form or order the movement takes. Practice among first-class players varies from one waggle of the club to Sandy Herd's famous seventeen. (I once counted them.)

My own preference is for a manner of addressing the ball that wastes little time. Having decided upon the club to use and the shot to play before stepping up to the ball, I can see no reason for taking any more time in the address than is necessary to measure one's distance from the ball and to line up the shot. The more one fiddles around arranging the position, the more likely one is to be beset by doubts that produce tension and strain.

It is far easier to maintain a perfect relaxation if one keeps continuously in motion, never becoming still and set. It sounds farfetched, I know, but I have had a few players tell me that after forming the habit of taking great pains in addressing the ball, they reached the point where they simply could not take the club back.

I liked to approach any shot from behind the ball. I think it is easier to get a picture of the shot and to line it up properly from this angle than from any other. Ordinarily, coming up from behind, I stopped a little short of what my final position would be. From there, I grounded the club behind the ball and looked toward the objective. The club gave me a sense of my distance from the ball, looking down the fairway gave me the line, while my left foot swung into position; one waggle was begun while the right foot moved back to its place; when the club returned to the ground behind the ball, there was a little forward twist of the hips and the backswing began. I felt most comfortable and played better golf when the movement was continuous. Whenever I hesitated or took a second waggle, I could look for trouble.

The little twist of the hips is a valuable aid in starting the swing smoothly, because it assists in breaking up any tension that may have crept in. Often referred to as the "forward press," it has been regarded by many as the result of a movement of the hands. In actual fact, the hands have nothing to do with it; the movement is in the body and knees, and its chief function is to assure a smooth start of the swing by setting the body in motion. Without it, the inclination is strong to pick the club up with the hands and arms, without bringing the trunk into use.

I do not think it wise to prescribe any definite number of waggles. That depends too much upon how long is required for the player to settle into a comfortable position; but it is important to make the movement easy, smooth, and comfortable, and to form the habit of getting the thing done without too much fussing and worry. In many cases, it will help to determine for a while to just step up to the ball and hit it.

9   THE POSITION OF THE HEAD

Someone once asked me if I was conscious of looking at the ball with my left eye rather than with my right. I replied that I was not, and that if I looked at the ball with either eye, it was a habit of such long standing that I no longer thought about it. "But," the man insisted, "I noticed that you and Walter Hagen and a good many of the other fellows held your heads in such a position that you appeared to be looking at the ball with the left eye. Surely, there must have been some reason for or advantage to be derived from the practice. I should like to know what it was."

I confessed that the position of my head when preparing to hit a golf ball was entirely instinctive. I began to do it long before I ever gave a thought to style or the mechanics of the stroke. I believe the same thing to have been true in Hagen's case. But several years ago I did have demonstrated to me the importance of the head position in its effect upon the rest of the stroke. I have never attached much importance to the "master eye" theory. I don't think it makes any difference which of a man's eyes is the stronger or whether he gazes at any particular point on the cover of the ball. All that he needs is to be able to measure the distance and to locate accurately the ball's position. I am told that he can do this better with two eyes than with one.

Back in 1927, it happened that Joe Kirkwood and I were on the same ship going to St. Andrews for the British Open. The captain of the vessel was kind enough to rig up a driving net for us on the upper deck, and every day Joe and I would go up to hit a few balls. The practice was of no value, even with a gentle roll of the ship, but it did serve to prevent our hands becoming tender. But hammering balls into a net is a dull business at best, and finally Joe began to do some of his famous trick shots and, of course, I tried to follow him. Naturally, there were very few I could accomplish without more practice than we had time for.

But one series of shots that Joe introduced to me shed a good bit of light on this question of the position of the head. These shots were played with an iron. Three balls would be placed on the mat, in line, and Joe would hit the first while looking directly behind him, the second while looking into the eye of an observer standing directly across the ball from him, and the third while looking in the direction in which the flag or the objective would lie. That looked fairly simple, after locating the first ball, so I had a go at it. After a few trials, I could hit the first ball, looking down the deck away from the canvas, and the second, looking at Joe standing at the other end of the mat, but the third, looking into the canvas in the direction of the flag, I could never hit, nor even make a respectable pass at it. With my chin to the front, I found it impossible to turn my hips or to swing the club back at all. The most I could do was to lift the club up and hack at the ball.

Alex Morrison, the famous teacher, more than anyone else, I think, has harped upon the "chin-back" idea. I am convinced that it is sound, for it places the head in a position where it will not tie up the rest of the body, either on the backswing or in the act of hitting the ball. Whenever you see a leading golfer hit a ball, watch his head. You will find that he either starts his swing with his head cocked a bit backward, or else he turns it for a few inches as the club goes back, and it won't make any difference whether he is "left-eyed" or "right-eyed."

10   "REACHING" FOR THE BALL

I wonder if the average golfer, while he is planting his feet and contorting his body preparatory to sending off one of his screaming drives, ever stops to think about the trouble he is starting for himself. I wonder if he ever conjures up in his mind a picture of any first-class golfer making the same preparations. If he does, I wonder if he thinks there is something supernatural, something unattainable, in the easy attitude, the graceful poise of the accomplished professional.

Addressing a golf ball would seem to be a simple matter; that is, to the uninitiated who cannot appreciate that a golf ball can hold more terrors than a spacious auditorium packed with people. Yet the 99%10 per cent who find golf a mysteriously difficult game apparently pack as much tension, strain, and other unnatural elements as possible into the act of merely making ready to swing the club. Watch any good pro walk up to a ball and prepare to sock it. He steps lightly up to his place; he falls easily into position; he stands with his body comfortably erect; he does not reach out for the ball; in short, he appears in every detail perfectly at ease and relaxed.

The handicap man, on the other hand, goes through the same process in an entirely different way. He fusses around with his feet trying to find the best place for each of them. When he thinks that he has placed them properly, he proceeds to plant them firmly, to root them immovably into the ground. He then bends low over the ball and stretches out until he can reach to a distance he thinks will enable him to hit it. In all this, there is a complete restriction of his muscles that makes it impossible for him to relax after the swing once gets under way.

Confidence that he knows what he is about has a lot to do with the easy attitude characteristic of the first-class professional, but I should not be surprised if the handicap player would soon find reason for a little more confidence in his own ability if he would imitate the nonchalance of his more capable brother. Let him stroll up to the shot more or less casually, keep his feet closer together, his body more erect, and in a natural carriage and posture try to lose some of the tension which comes of trying to set himself in just such a way.

I have seen worlds of trouble caused by bending the left arm too much at address, this in its turn being made necessary by bending the body over too far. The evil of this posture is that in the act of hitting, when the left arm straightens out, the head and shoulders must be elevated to accommodate the greater stretch of the arms. Since the head and shoulders are the anchor points of the stroke, it is not hard to see that such a happening upsets the whole business and leaves the arc of the swing dangling in midair without a resting point.

To lean over and reach for the ball has two other effects that are definitely harmful. First, the reaching produces a tension in the muscles of the forearms; and second, the excessive bend at the waist considerably lessens the player's ability to turn his hips freely. Both are bad, but it seems to me that the tying up of the hips is by far the worse, because it is in the use of the muscles in the waist and back that the average golfer is most deficient. It is safe to say that not one player in a thousand turns his hips enough.

Whatever virtue there may be in getting up close to the ball, so far as concerns the possibility that the eyes may thus be better placed to line up the shot, may be disregarded. The important fact is that the more erect posture makes it easier for all members and muscles of the body to cooperate in a smooth and powerful stroke.

11   AN INSIDIOUS HABIT

One reason golf is such an exasperating game is that a thing learned is so easily forgotten, and we find ourselves struggling year after year with faults we had discovered and corrected time and again. But no correction seems to have a permanent effect, and as soon as our minds become busy with another part of the swing, the old defection pops up again to annoy us.

This is especially true with respect to placing the ball in the position of address. Apparently of little importance, this is one of the most vital considerations in hitting a golf ball, not that one position is correct for every player, but because for each player there is one position which, with the peculiarities of his method, enables him to hit the ball most easily and most effectively.

In my particular case, this position happens to be at a point about opposite the middle of my left foot, and this is true when using any club for almost any kind of shot. Of course, the exigencies of a peculiar situation may alter this position to some extent, but normally it remains the same. With the ball in this forward position, all the power of the stroke can be applied behind the ball; there is no additional tension and loss of power because of a position which requires the player to hold back in order to meet the ball squarely.

It is not difficult to see that if the swing is adjusted to strike the ball in a certain position, even a slight variation in the position of the ball, the swing remaining the same, will cause an error in hitting. No golfer needs to be told what ruinous results may follow from even a small mistake. Taking the ball an inch too soon or an inch too late may throw it many yards off line at the end of its flight.

Placing the ball at address should always receive minute attention. Too many times we step up confidently and carelessly to play a shot, and fall readily into a position that feels comfortable and is, we think, the accustomed attitude. Without giving the thing a thought, we hit the shot and are at a loss to explain the pull or slice that results. A tiny error is enough, and it is very easy to overlook.

At Winged Foot in the 1929 National Open Championship, I played my irons better than at any other time in my life—that is, in important competition—and I don't think I should have done so had I been left entirely to my own devices. On the morning of the first day, I went out on the East Course to warm up a bit before starting. After hitting a few drives that went off all right, I dropped back to a four-iron, a club I used in practice as a sort of indicator to the prospective behavior of all its companions.

With it I hit shot after shot, trying everything I could think of, but all went to the right of the objective except a few that I tried to keep straight by a vigorous roll of the right hand. These were just as far off line in the other direction. This was not exactly a pleasant situation to confront immediately before starting a tournament.

Finally, T. N. Bradshaw of Atlanta, who made the trip with me and who was watching my practice, spoke up. Brad had played with me at least as much as anyone, and he knew my game. A suggestion from him could never be out of place.

"I think you are playing the ball too far back, Bob," he said quietly.

I myself did not think so, but I was in a mood to try anything. So I played the next few a bit farther forward and from that time had no more trouble. This gave me one more thing to think about, but it was worth more than all the others.

A slight change of position is hard for the player himself to detect, especially if he plays for any appreciable time in that way. But to move the ball interferes not at all with the swing. To try a different position endangers none of the elements of touch, timing, or rhythm. And very often it will be found to be the exact adjustment required. It is impossible to contend that the same relative positions of ball and feet are proper for every player. But if anyone is off his game, it will do no harm to experiment—to shift the ball nearer the left foot to correct a slice, and nearer the right foot to correct a hook. If it works, it is the simplest specific that can be given.

CHAPTER THREE

1 THE PURPOSE OF THE BACKSWING   41

2 ORIGINATING THE BACKSWING   42

3 ARGUMENTS FOR A LONG BACKSWING   43

4 ROLL OF THE LEFT FOOT   45

5 COCKING THE WRISTS   46

6 THE POSITION AT THE TOP   47

7 SHIFTING THE WEIGHT   50

Starting Back

CHAPTER THREE

1 THE PURPOSE OF THE BACKSWING

It is often urged that a person playing golf who worries about how to take the club back, how to start it down, and what to do at this stage and at that, ultimately loses sight of the only important thing he has to do—to hit the ball. We, who write on the game and those who attempt to teach it, are told often enough that we should give more attention to the contact stage and less to the details of the preparatory movements.

It is true, of course, that it is not impossible to hit an occasional good shot even though all the teachings and practice of the experts in fundamentals may be disregarded; but one who takes the long-range viewpoint cannot fail to appreciate that the basis of consistent and reliable performance is good form. There are certain actions that must take place during the act of hitting if the ball is to be struck with accuracy and power. A haphazard, uninformed player once in a while may find himself in position to complete these actions, but he cannot hope to compete successfully with the man whose sound swing carries him time after time into this position.

The downward or hitting stroke is intended to culminate in a well-timed, powerful contact between club head and ball. There is no way to argue that the successful accomplishment of this purpose is not the most important part of the stroke; but the backswing has for its purpose the establishment of a perfectly balanced, powerful position at the top of the swing from which the correct actions of the downstroke can flow rhythmically without the need for interference or correction. In the end, on the basis of consistent reproduction of the successful action, the preparatory movements become just as important as the actual hitting—the entire swing, a sequence of correct positions, following naturally and comfortably one after the other.

2   ORIGINATING THE BACKSWING

I have always favored a method that brings the club back well away from the line of play—around the body, if you please—because such a stroke has the advantage of greater power without sacrificing accuracy, if it is executed correctly. The most striking difference between the expert and the good businessman golfer is in the use of the hips and body, and any attempt to swing the club in a more upright arc—straight back from the ball—is likely to discourage still further the correct use of these members. This effort is likely to produce a swing accomplished by the arms alone, leaving an important source of power entirely neglected.

The moderate flatness of the swing that I like must result from a correct body-turn, and not from manipulation of the club by the hands and wrists. Many players begin the backswing with a sudden pronation of the left wrist that whips the club sharply around the legs, opening the face very quickly. This is just as bad as a swing straight back, carrying the arms away from the player's body.

The initial movement of the club away from the ball should result from forces originating in the left side. The real takeoff is from the left foot, starting the movement of the body. The hands and arms very soon pick it up, but the proper order at the very beginning is body, arms, and lastly club head. It is always easier to continue a motion than to begin it; this order has the virtue of originating the hip-turn; it goes a long way toward assuring a proper windup of the hips during the backswing.

It is easy to think of the golf swing entirely in terms of the club head, and, after getting set, more or less painfully, to begin the backswing by some sort of movement of the hands to start the club head going. Regardless of what this movement may be, it is bound to result in neglect of the all-important turning movement.

The period of contact between club and ball is practically instantaneous. To move the club head backward and forward as much as possible along the line of flight means very, very little; all that is necessary is that it be properly aligned and moving in the right direction at one particular instant—when it strikes the ball.

3   ARGUMENTS FOR A LONG BACKSWING

Probably the most important and useful conception for the golfer is that of swinging, ever swinging, as opposed to the idea of forceful hitting. This is the chief reason that relaxation is stressed so endlessly, for tension impedes a free swing, and often checks the blow before the ball has been struck. A true swing, after building up speed, offers no counterforce diminishing power, but makes efficient use of all the energy that has been stored up.

One of the characteristics of the true swing, and the one that most often escapes the inexpert player, is the ample sweep of the backward windup. The average golfer, partly because he is unfamiliar with the movements that will accommodate a long backswing, and partly because he does not trust himself to go so far, almost always favors a short, hacking stroke. Quickly back and quickly down, employing a sudden acceleration almost amounting to a jerk, there is scarcely any chance of obtaining power or accuracy.

The most usual argument in favor of a backswing of good length is that it allows a longer arc and more time to attain the maximum club head speed at the instant of contact. But there are others of at least equal force. It is certain that the more gradual acceleration made possible by the longer backswing is bound to make the swing much smoother and less likely to be yanked out of its groove; also, it is certain that it makes it possible to attain an equal speed with less sudden effort and therefore less likelihood of introducing contrary forces detracting from the power of the stroke.

The whole force of a sound swing is not dissipated at the ball. It is desirable that the blow should be directed through the ball, and not merely at it. The feeling is that the club head, having built up its full speed, is merely floating through the last little space immediately prior to contact. The moment one feels an awareness of having to hit—the need of an extra effort—the hands tighten upon the club, resistance is set up, and the motion is slowed down rather than accelerated.

The easy, and usually graceful, pose in which the correct golf swing comes to an end is the result of this relaxed swinging. Muscles that have not been tightened in the effort of hitting do not tighten up to stop the club. When the swing has passed through the ball, the work has been done, the impulse is withdrawn, and the momentum of the club simply draws a compliant body around to the finish of the swing.

If we liken the backswing of a golf club to the extension of a coil spring, or the stretching of a rubber band, I think we shall not be very far off our mark. The greater the extension or stretching, the greater the force of the return. In the golf swing, every inch added to the backward windup, up to the limit at which the balance of the body can be easily maintained, represents additional stored energy available to increase the power of the downswing. It may be possible for the player with a comparatively short windup to make up this difference by an extraordinary hitting effort, but he will never be able to do so without more than a proportionate loss in smoothness and precision.

It seems to me likely that too much stress has been laid upon the desirability of compactness in the swing, especially when the impression is that such compactness demands an abbreviated stroke. Many players have come to believe that a short backswing, by eliminating some of the body turn, simplifies the stroke to such an extent that grave errors will be avoided. I have always held the contrary view, and am convinced that a great many more shots are spoiled by a swing that is too short than by one that is too long, and this applies in the use of every club, from the driver down to and including the putter.

The one quality a golf swing must have is smoothness. The acceleration from the top must be gradual, and the motion must be unhurried and free from any sudden or jerky movements. In order to accomplish it in this manner, the club head must have plenty of time to gather speed before it reaches the ball. It is apparent that the longer the arc through which the club travels, the less need there will be for any abnormal expenditure of energy at any one particular instant. The long path affords plenty of space for building up velocity from the zero point at the top to a maximum at the moment the ball is met.

4   ROLL OF THE LEFT FOOT

Many players, for one reason or another, form the habit of arriving at the top of the swing with too much of their weight supported by the left leg. This is usually evidenced by the heel of the left foot being firmly planted on the ground at this stage. Not only in such a swing is the player prevented from shifting his hips forward as he begins to unwind, but the necessity of maintaining his balance will always force him to fall back upon his right foot as he swings through.

The raising of the left heel during the backswing must not be considered to be an end in itself; rather, is it to be looked upon as the result of handling the backward windup of the body in a correct fashion. The body simply turns, with the weight either moving back toward the right foot, or, if enough of it is already there, without any lateral shift whatever, and the heel comes up as the leg action accommodates the turning movement.

One thing should be emphasized—that there must be no pivoting on the toe of the left foot. The weight supported by this leg at the start of the backswing should be felt to roll across the foot until it is resting upon the inside of the ball of the foot and the great toe. The player who swings his foot around and pirouettes upon his toe until the entire sole of the shoe is exposed to the hole is guilty of a very serious mistake. By doing so, he puts his left leg entirely out of commission and otherwise upsets any possibility of correct body movement.

5   COCKING THE WRISTS

In any full swing, correctly performed, the trunk will begin to unwind while the hands and club are still going back. This order of movement has the effect of accomplishing two very important results. First, of course, it causes the hip-turn to lead the downstroke and so makes the power generated by the reverse turn of the body usable in the form of club head momentum. But equally important is the effect of completing the cocking of the wrists. This is accomplished as the wrists give to the pull of the hips in one direction and of the club head moving in the other. As the downstroke begins, one should have the feeling of leaving the club head at the top.

The habit of maintaining this order in a full swing came to me quite naturally. I suppose if it had not, I should never have reached the stage where I should care enough about golf to worry with it. But for years I was a very poor mashie-niblick player simply because I was inclined to be a bit wooden in my wrists when playing the shorter strokes. The abbreviated backswing was not enough to free me of this restraint. I was getting enough wrist movement to avoid shanking, but not enough to assure the crisp downward blow needed for good pitching.

An ample cocking of the wrists, and the retention of the greater part of this angle for use in the hitting area is not only important for good timing and increasing the speed of the club head; it is absolutely necessary in order to enable the player to

THE POSITION AT THE TOP

strike downward and so produce backspin. When the angle between the left arm and the shaft of the club becomes open too
early in the downstroke, the club head at this point will be too
low and the subsequent arc will be too flat.

6 THE POSITION AT THE TOP

There is no part of the golf swing that consists of one simple
movement. The whole thing is a process of blending, cor-
relating, and harmonizing simple movements until smooth, rhythmic motion is achieved. When actually swinging a club, there
is no way to complete the body turn and wrist movement sepa-
rately, having done with one before the other is commenced. But
a simple little exercise can be performed to illustrate the nature
of each.

Let the player grip the club in the manner I have described
and address the ball. Then, without moving his body, let him
raise the club with his hands and arms until his hands are about
opposite his chest and well away from his body, and his wrists
are cocked so that the shaft of the club passes over his right
shoulder. Then, keeping his eye on the ball and his head steady,
let him turn his body about the spine as an axis. When he has
accomplished a full turn, he will find himself approximately in
the position he would like to reach at the top of his swing. He
has executed the two essential movements that are blended in
the correct backswing.

Now there are a number of important things to be watched
in the position at the top of the swing. It is possible to write
many pages on this phase of the stroke. But the one feature I
have in mind now is the one the duffer ignores entirely, and yet
it has everything to do with the success of the stroke.

At the top of the swing the shaft of the club, which for the
long shots is in a position approximately in a horizontal plane,
should at the same time be pointing to a spot slightly to the
right of the object at which the player is aiming. This will be

found to be a uniform practice among the best professional golfers. It is the result of swinging the club back to the top, rather than lifting it up as so many beginners do.

Now, from this position it is important in what manner the club is started downward. The necessary elevation of the hands at the top of the swing draws the right elbow away from the ribs, where it should have remained until the last possible moment. The elbow is not, however, lifted into the air aimlessly; the right forearm should point obliquely, almost vertically, toward the ground and be drawn away from the side only by as much as may be necessary to accommodate a full swing of the club.

Many players advance this far with fair success; but the next step usually trips them. The almost irresistible impulse now, when all is in readiness to wallop the ball, is to allow the right hand too much freedom. Immediately that unruly member, which has to be watched continually, whips the club over the right shoulder toward the front of the player, whence it must approach the ball from outside the line of flight. Whether a smothered hook or a bad slice results, depends only upon whether the club face is shut or open when it reaches the ball. If anything like a decent shot results, it may be ascribed to pure accident.

The proper start down from the top position I have described is in the direction in which the grip end of the shaft is pointing. Since the head end of the club is pointing slightly to the right of the objective aimed at, the grip end will be directed away from the vertical plane in which the ball rests. In other words, instead of immediately beginning to approach the line of flight as the downward stroke commences, the club head should be made at first to drop away from that line.

The importance of this movement cannot be overestimated. The right elbow quickly drops back into place close to the side of the body, and the player is in a compact position ready to deliver a blow squarely at the back of the ball. There is no possibility of cutting across the shot.

So that the action may be visualized more clearly, let us imagine that we are standing directly in front of the player, looking toward him in a direction at right angles to the line of play, that the movement takes place all in one plane, and that we can see only the shaft of the club and the player's left arm, from the shoulder down.

At the beginning of the backswing, when the grip upon the club is light and the wrist and forearm relaxed, the motion originated by the turn of the hips and the movement of the arm causes a break in the approximately straight line from the left shoulder to the club head. From our point of observation, this break is toward our left as the hand moves in that direction and the relaxed wrist joint flexes back toward the ball.

This is the drag so clearly defined in slow-motion pictures, and it is the beginning of the leisurely slinging characteristic of the swings of all good players. As the backswing progresses farther, the club head catches up, passes through a point where the straight line from the shoulder to club head is restored, and continues on in the action that gradually completes the cocking of the wrists. The full amount of this cock is indicated to us when the angle between the straight left arm and the shaft of the club is most acute.

An interesting point is that apparently it does not make much difference where, within limits, of course, this angle of greatest cock is reached. The player who indulges in a full backswing usually exhibits this angle at its most acute stage at what might be called the top of the backswing just before his arm starts down. But the man with a shorter backswing often diminishes or closes the angle still more after his arms have definitely begun their downward sweep.

But wherever precisely the maximum cock is obtained, it is important that the angle should not begin to open at the very beginning of the downstroke. Many players, in order to accomplish what they conceive to be the desirable act of throwing the club head at the ball, open this angle too quickly. They arrive at a point where they want to hit, and discover that they have little left to hit with. As soon as the left arm and the shaft of the club are again on a straight line, the wrist-cock has been used up, and only a disastrous rolling of the shoulders can be used in its place. Unquestionably, the increasing speed and momentum of the club must open this angle some, but as much of it as possible ought to be saved for hitting.

7   SHIFTING THE WEIGHT

It is my definite opinion that there need be no shifting of weight from left foot to right during the backstroke. I have examined numbers of photographs of the very best players and I have been able to find no case in which such a shifting was perceptible; but there should occur during the hitting stroke a pronounced shift from right to left—a shift that does not follow the club, or pass smoothly along coincident with its progress, but is executed quickly, and leads the arms and club all the way through.

The more expert players stand almost erect when addressing the ball. Rarely does one see a really first-rate player bend or stoop over the ball. His body curves only very slightly and his weight is equally apportioned to each foot, and, if it is possible, evenly distributed over the area of each. In other words, he stands neither upon his heels nor upon his toes. From this position, the proper body action is purely a turn or pivot with no shifting or sway whatever.

The downswing or hitting stroke presents another picture. There is a shift here, but there is no sway, and the difference is what the average golfer wants to understand. It is this: the weight shift which is proper is a shift of the hips—a lateral movement of the middle part of the body that does not alter the location of the head and shoulders with respect to the ball; the sway, which is improper, is a forward movement of the entire body, that sends the head and shoulders forward, too, and tends to upset the player's balance.

There are two common methods of handling the weight improperly. The more damage is caused by settling most of the weight upon the left foot at the top of the swing; a beginner nearly always has a liking for this. Although we may sometimes overlook the root of the trouble, the result is a familiar sight. The effort of hitting always throws the weight violently back upon the right foot. The player falls away from the ball, his left foot flies up into the air, and his balance is completely lost. The other method, too, we have often seen, when in the back-swing the player draws his entire body backward, and finds himself poised at the top with his entire weight upon his right foot and his left leg completely straight. This beginning ends in a despairing lunge that usually carries the ball nowhere.

If we examine the swings of several golfers, even with the naked eye, it is easy enough to tell whether the weight transference has been a sway or a shift. One characteristic of the proper body action, that is to say, the shift, is that the left leg is straight at and after impact. If you want to know why this is, you have only to look at the line, which marks the left side of the body. It has been lengthened, without lifting the head, by holding the shoulder back while the left hip goes forward. The characteristic of the sway, located again in the left leg, is a decided bend of the left knee in the same area; the entire weight of the body being thrown forward prevents the straightening of the left leg so that either the knee bends or the player falls flat on his face.

CHAPTER FOUR

1   DEVELOPING A STYLE   55

2   THE MOST IMPORTANT MOVEMENT   56

3   AN IMPORTANT FAULT   57

4   USING THE BODY   58

5   HITTING DOWN ON THE BALL   60

6   INSIDE-OUT?   62

7   USING YOUR LEGS   64

8   LOOKING UP   65

Starting Down

CHAPTER FOUR

I DEVELOPING A STYLE

More than fine-spun theories, the average golfer needs something to give him a clearer conception of what he should try to do with the club head. The golf swing is a set or series of movements that must be closely correlated. The smallest change in any one will make a difference in one or more of the others, and although for consistent, high-class performance there can be only a small deviation in any particular, it still is a fact, and always will be so, that there are more ways than one of swinging a golf club effectively.

I do not intend to argue against the development of a good sound method, but I do believe that this method should be put together with due regard for the requirements and swing preferences of the individual. I think also that before a player should begin to worry about the finer points of form, he should play enough to know what his preferences are.

When we speak of a sound swing or of good form, we mean nothing more than that the possessor of either has simplified his swing to the point where errors are less likely to creep in, and that he is able consistently to bring his club against the ball in the correct hitting position. We talk, think, and write so much about the details of the stroke that we sometimes lose sight of the one thing that is all-important—hitting the ball. It is conceivable that a person could perform all sorts of contortions and yet bring the club into correct relation to the ball at impact, in which case a good shot must result. The only reason for discussing method and form at all is to find a way to make it easier for the player to achieve this correct relationship. In a crude way, he might do it only occasionally; in a finished, sound, controlled way, he will be able to do it consistently and with assurance.

Ultraslow motion pictures made by the Professional Golfers Association show one point of comparison of the methods of Harry Vardon and myself that demonstrates how one motion or position depends upon another, and how after all, it is only the contact between club and ball that matters. The pictures show that at the instant of impact, Vardon's hands are perceptibly behind the ball, and that he has whipped the clubhead forward to make contact, whereas at the corresponding instant in my swing, the hands are slightly in front of the ball and the club head is being pulled through. Years of play and experience had told each of us that we must handle the club in this way in order to bring the club face into the correct position; and while we may be thinking of some other part of the stroke, subconsciously, through our sense of touch, we bring the club head around in the way we have learned produces a good shot. The reason for this difference is found in the slightly different positions of our hands on the club, my left hand being slightly more on top of the shaft than Vardon's. If either should meet the ball in the same way as the other, a bad shot must inevitably result.

This is the sense every golfer must develop. The beginner ought to keep always before him the determination to put the club against the ball in the correct position. It is not easy when form is lacking, but it is the surest way to cause form to be more easily acquired. The expert player corrects subconsciously; some instantaneous telegraphic system tells him, just as he begins to hit, that something is wrong; and at the last instant a muscle that may not always function perfectly will do so in a sufficient number of cases for it to be well worth its keep.

2 THE MOST IMPORTANT MOVEMENT

If the grip be left out of the picture on the ground that it is in truth a preliminary, and we can assume that this is correct, then I should say that the most important movement of the swing would be to start the downswing by beginning the unwinding of the hips. It is possible to play good golf without a straight left arm; it is possible to do so using a square, closed, or open stance; and one may get along with a short and fast backswing if there are compensating virtues. But there can be no power, and very little accuracy or reliability, in a swing in which the left hip does not lead the downstroke.

One sees any number of players who take the club back almost in a vertical arc, thereby violating the principles of the true swing. In other words, instead of swinging it back, they lift it up over their shoulders; but a lot of them, because they initiate the downswing by beginning the turn of the hips before they move anything else, manage to play good golf.

No matter how perfect the backswing may have been, if the hands, or the arms, or the shoulders start the downward movement, the club immediately loses the guidance of the body movement, and the benefit of the power the muscles of the waist and back could have contributed. When this happens, the turn of the body during the backswing becomes entirely useless, and the club finds itself in midair, actuated by a pair of hands and arms having no effective connection with anything solid. I think we may well call this the most important movement of the swing.

3 AN IMPORTANT FAULT

Hitting with the right hand from the top of the swing ruins as many shots as any other single fault. By forcing the downswing out beyond its proper groove, and by using up the cock of the wrists too quickly, it can lead to almost anything from a smothered hook to a full-fledged shank. When the right hand takes charge at the top, there is no possibility of approaching the ball from inside the line of play—and nearly every golfer is inclined to do this, especially when he is trying to hit hard.

The remedy or preventive involves two main intentions: first, to relax the right arm as completely as possible during the backswing, and second, to begin the downswing at a moderate pace, no matter how hard you intend to hit. There is nothing complex in this prescription, yet I am certain that it will prove to be of considerable aid to any kind of player.

Relaxing the right arm keeps this member from lifting or picking up the club from the ball, and so beginning the swing in a too upright plane. It also puts the job of swinging the club squarely up to the left side of the body, and thus forces it to push the club back. But, of equal importance, while the right arm is relaxed, the right elbow is not likely to heave into space away from the side. It will remain tucked in close—but not tensed—until the upper reaches of the swing draw it away.

In this way, the relaxed right arm is exceedingly helpful in arriving at a correct hitting position. It assures a swing rather than a lifting action; it encourages a full windup of the hips; it allows the club to move back so that it can be swung down on the inside; and it leaves the left hand in control, as it should be.

To keep constantly in mind that the start down should be leisurely is almost a necessity, for here is the means of keeping the swing in gear at a crucial stage. When one has arrived at the top, and prepared for the return, the inclination is strong to let everything go in an effort to use every ounce of power. This is where the right hand can cause a lot of trouble if it is used too soon. But if one merely thinks of dropping the right elbow back to the side of the body, while the wrists retain their cocking, and of doing this at a leisurely pace, a proper start will be made and speed can be built up and used in an effective way. It is this action here that makes it possible to hit along the line of flight or across it from the inside.

4   USING THE BODY

One reason, or excuse, offered by the average golfer for a bad slice is that he got his body in too soon. Since any such idea is bound to discourage an ample use of the hips and back (exactly the point wherein I believe the average player is most remiss), and because, in nine cases out of ten it is entirely wrong, I think a little consideration of the body movement in the downswing may be helpful.

Motion pictures of numbers of our best professionals disclose three common characteristics that are important to a discussion of this particular point. First, the hips begin to unwind—that is, to turn back toward the ball—even before the club has reached the end of its backward travel; second, the left heel returns to the ground very early in the downstroke while the hands are at shoulder level or above; and third, at impact the hips have turned through the address position, and at this point the lower part of the body fronts almost toward the hole. Thus, it is impossible to escape the conclusion that the unwinding of the hips in the correct swing is very rapid indeed.

I have often observed precisely the same action in a baseball pitcher warming up close to the stands before a game. There is no doubt that the quick twist of the hips beginning the throwing movement supplies important momentum that increases both speed and endurance. If a pitcher were to eliminate his hip movement, or retard it to such a degree that it would be useless, he would be a very weary young man at the end of nine innings.

The momentum obtained by the golfer, when the unwinding of his hips leads the hitting movement, is no less important to him than to the baseball pitcher. For one thing, it makes it possible for him to attain a much greater speed at impact with appreciably less effort.

I tried many times, in testing this idea, to turn my hips too rapidly in hitting a full drive. I found this to be impossible so long as I observed the rudiments of good form. Indeed, I was able to trace many errors to slowing down or stopping the hip-turn too quickly.

The average golfer usually experiences trouble for one of two reasons. Either he omits the forward movement or shift of the hips that must precede and blend in with the beginning of the unwinding, or he moves his whole body, including head and shoulders, in a sort of lunge at the ball. He cannot hope to do other than cut across the ball if he holds the greater part of his weight upon his right leg, or falls back upon it as he brings his club down.

In the correct swing, starting down, the hips should shift forward slightly before any noticeable unwinding takes place. I like Abe Mitchell's expression that "the player should move freely beneath himself." In other words, the head and shoulders should not accompany the hips in this initial movement.

I have often referred to the stretch that I feel up the left side and arm, from hip to hand, as the result of leading the downswing with the hip-turn while the club is still going back. Now the hands drop almost vertically downward, starting the right shoulder moving below the left, from which point the swing is able to pass through the ball on a line approximately straight toward the objective.

Handling the several movements in this way, I have not found it possible to turn the hips too quickly. Whenever a player gets his body into the shot in any way greatly different from this, he is wrong whether he does it too soon or not.

5   HITTING DOWN ON THE BALL

Expert players have discovered that the maximum length from the tee, or when playing a ball lying well in the fairway, can be obtained by causing the club to strike the ball at or slightly in front of the lowest point in the arc of the swing. The notion that a golf ball can be made to fly carrying overspin is pure fantasy, but when the ball is struck squarely in the back with the club moving parallel to the ground, or slightly upward, a minimum of backspin results. A ball so struck will fly in an arching trajectory so that it will still have some run left in it when it returns to the ground. A ball struck in this way will also have a greater capability of boring into a headwind.

This, of course, demands a degree of control on the part of the player that is not to be expected of the average golfer. In most cases, the matter of control is far more important than length, and backspin is a steadying influence upon the flight of the ball. The average golfer should do his utmost to learn to play every shot in this controlled manner. Above all, he should be convinced that he cannot lift the ball from a cuppy or downhill lie by striking upward; on the contrary, he must rely upon backspin to cause the ball to become airborne.

Excepting only the drive and the long shots from the fairway, when maximum length is desired, every stroke in the game should be played so that the club meets the ball while still in its descending arc. The angle of descent varies from the woods that merely shave the ground to the pitching club moving slabs of turf; but the spin imparted by the downward blow is needed to control the flight of the ball.

The player who tries, with any wood club, to get a ball up from a cuppy lie by getting the club under it in order to hit it upward is doomed to disappointment. He must either strike the ground first, or missing that, with the club coming up, hit the ball on top. This kind of shot can be played only by smashing the ball down so that the spin will cause it to rise. This is why, as you may have noticed, it is easier to play from a tight lie on level ground than on an upward slope. The need for the descending arc remains the same, but the slope, which at first blush would seem a help, makes the handling of the body movement more difficult.

The average golfer realizing that he cannot get the ball up from close lies, nor apply a really effective backspin with any club, until he learns to swing so that the club will strike a descending blow, should begin to find out what he must do to accomplish this result consistently. Merely to hit the ball down is not enough. Indeed, almost every duffer begins by hitting down; but at the same time he cuts across the ball viciously. Keeping most of his weight on his left foot, or shifting it there during the backswing, when he begins to hit, he falls back upon his right foot, and brings the club across the line of play from the outside. Naturally, this will not do. In order to be effective, the downward blow must be directed approximately along the line upon which the ball is expected to travel.

Of course, in order to explain fully how any particular shot may be played correctly, one must describe the whole of the correct swing. But here are the main points which directly affect the direction of the blow:

The first should be to see that the distribution of weight at the top of the swing is such that in hitting through, the player will not have to fall back upon his right foot in order to maintain his balance; this means that a preponderance of weight must not rest upon the left leg at this point. An approximately equal division between the two feet is correct, and this can be arrived at by starting with an equal division in the address position, and completing the backswing by a simple turn of the trunk without transference either way.

After the windup of the hips has been completed in the backswing, the unwinding must start before the club head begins its return to the ball; and at the same time the hips must shift slightly forward in order to move the center of the swing in that direction. In no case must this center be allowed to move backward, for then the ball must be struck upward, or very much across.

This much, done properly, gives a fair assurance that a descending blow can be delivered; but it can be undone in an instant if the hands begin to move the club too soon. The angle between the left arm and the shaft of the club has been made more acute by the pull of the left hip, as it began unwinding, against the club still swinging up. If, in overeagerness to hit, the player should throw the club head from the top, and thus straighten out the angle at which his wrists have been cocked, his hope of hitting down passes immediately. The arc of his downswing moves straightway beyond its proper groove, and the only chance of bringing it to the ball lies in a sort of lifting, shoveling action, performed mainly with the shoulders and arms. This is what a great many players do when they try to hit unusually hard.

The cocking of the wrists must be retained through the early stages of the downswing; the momentum must come from the unwinding of the hips. At the same time, the right elbow must move down close to the side of the body, and the swing must remain on the player's side of the ball, from where it can direct the club in hitting approximately along the line of flight.

6   INSIDE-OUT?

Should the club at impact be traveling from the inside to out, or parallel to the line of play?" The answer is certainly that when a straight flying shot is desired, the ideal condition is met if the club, when it makes contact with the ball, is moving precisely along the line of intended flight, with its face exactly square, or perpendicular, to the line of play. A deviation in either the alignment of the club face or in the direction of its motion must tend to drive the ball off line, or to impart a sidespin which will cause it to curve in its flight.

Players are advised to try to hit from inside-to-out because the tendency of most is to hit from outside-to-in, or cut across the ball. If they actually succeed in causing the club head to cross the ball location from inside the line of play toward the outside of this line, the chances are that an uncontrolled hook will result. The expert player, who is adept at club manipulation and sure of his swing, plays a controlled hook or draw in this way—that is, by directing his stroke slightly outward. But this is beyond the average golfer. If the latter can ever reach the point where he can swing straight through toward the objective, he will have little cause to complain.

It is always important in playing golf that there should be in the mind of the player a definite picture of what he intends to do with the club head. It is safe to say that a vast majority of the struggling multitude are able to conjure up no very accurate conception of the swing. As they stand before the ball, their minds are utterly confused with all the do's and don'ts they can think of, jumbled together. Even if a picture they might have should contain a few inaccuracies, still they would be better off than with no plan at all.

One thing that has led to trouble has been the effort made by so many to "throw the clubhead at the ball," especially when there has been trouble with slicing, a fault to which most inexpert players are addicted. It is never difficult to attribute a badly cut shot to late hitting—that is, to a failure to bring the face of the club around quickly enough—and the most obvious means of correction is by holding the hands back and whipping the club head through.

The chief trouble with this procedure is that it almost always exaggerates the mistake sought to be avoided, or results in smothering, which is worse. This is one place where the inside-out theory should be given a chance, not as a thing to be actually accomplished, but as an end toward which to strive in order to correct the slices.

The picture I like to have in mind is one of hitting directly along the line of flight, with the face of the club exactly squared to the hole, and in order to accomplish this ideal I have found it very helpful to "see" my hands slightly ahead of the club head at impact. The club face having opened during the backswing must, of course, be closed again coming down, but this operation can be and should be handled by the left hand without any necessity for holding the hands back. It is obviously impossible to hit from the inside out, or even along the line of flight, if the club head is allowed to get in front of the hands before the ball is struck.

Leo Diegel, when he was having one of his good days, was probably the most accurate iron player in the world. I saw him on occasions when each iron shot looked as though it would knock the flag out of the hole, and it was characteristic of Diegel on such an occasion that his hands were perceptibly ahead of the club. The impression one gained from watching him was that the club was being pulled through with the left side.

This hand-in-front picture automatically takes care of several things recognized as part and parcel of good form. This one idea, besides suggesting a blow in the right direction, also assures that the punch will be slightly downward, and that the weight of the body will flow forward into the stroke. The attempt to whip the club head through ahead of the hands usually sets the player back upon his right foot, a mistake which should never be allowed.

As in every other aspect of the golf stroke, exaggeration here must be avoided. There are players who actually do permit the club head to lag too far behind, but it will pay a person troubled with slicing to examine his swing and find out if he is not holding his hands and his body back too much. Among the expert players, it is not uncommon to find the hands as much as three or four inches beyond the ball at impact.

7   USING YOUR LEGS

One often sees a player who habitually allows the right leg to cave in as his club approaches the ball. This gives his swing a sort of loose-jointed, haphazard appearance and, of course, reduces to zero his chance of controlling his stroke or delivering a well-directed blow. But the fault is equally apparent in the left leg, for there he has made the mistake of accentuating the bend of the knee and failing to straighten the leg as he neared the ball. Once he learns to handle his left side correctly, he will not likely have trouble with his right.

The two most important things to watch in the leg movement are, first, that in starting down the bend of the knees should not be sufficient to cause any appreciable lowering of the head and shoulders; and, second, that as the club nears the ball, the legs should be ready to produce the upward thrust that means so much in power. To all who have studied motion pictures of the golf stroke, the semisquatting posture at which the player arrives when his hands are about waist high on the downstroke is familiar. From that point on, there takes place a straightening of the left leg that culminates suddenly in a powerful upward thrust immediately prior to contact. Inevitably, this movement tends to straighten the right leg as well.

The correct use of the legs is as important as anything in golf, for the expert player makes much of his connection with the ground. A golfer is no exception to the rule in athletics, placing such a high value upon substantial underpinning.

8 LOOKING UP

Golf is recognized as one of the more difficult games to play or teach. One reason for this is that each person necessarily plays by feel, and a feel is almost impossible to describe. Another reason is because certain things necessary to be done cannot be attacked directly, but must be made right while directing the attention to something else. It has been my experience that the admonition to hold the head still and keep the eye on the ball in most cases comes under this latter heading; for almost anyone, attempting to fix his eye upon the ball or to hold his head immovable, soon finds himself so full of tension that he is helpless.

I have occasionally run across a person who said that he was helped by selecting a particular point on the surface of the ball at which to look. But the pros and better amateurs will always tell you that they do not consciously fix their gaze upon any particular point nor, indeed, upon the ball at all. They are merely aware of the location of the ball. They are, no doubt, seeing it during the entire stroke, but they do not stare at it.

This is carried a step further by some of those who have noticed that the first-class player, in playing a normal stroke, keeps his head down for a perceptible interval after he strikes the ball. Some interpret this as an indication that there is an effort to keep the gaze upon the spot from which the ball has departed, in an effort to avoid looking up too quickly. Yet this is hardly ever the case. I doubt if one of these men would ever be aware that he had not the ball in sight from the moment his backswing began until the flight of the ball had ended or had carried beyond an obstruction where it was no longer visible.

The danger of looking up apparently becomes greater as the length of the shot becomes less. Rarely do you see an indication of looking up when the player is driving or playing an iron shot. Sometimes the head comes up and the shot is spoiled, but I think this is caused more by a resistance elsewhere in the stroke forcing the head away, than by failing to look at the ball. In other words, the head-lifting itself results from a mechanical fault, and does not itself start the trouble.

In chipping and putting there may be this difference. Within the hitting area is where the club is most likely to distract the eye; when playing a full shot, the club head is moving so fast that little interference is likely to result. On the putting green, however, the player's chief concern just before he begins his stroke is to align the face of his club exactly; and the head of the putter remains always before his eye. There is danger then of distracting, not so much his eye or gaze, but his attention from the ball.

I experienced a spell of bad putting that I finally determined was due solely to a habit of following the putter blade with my eye as it moved away from the ball. Of course, the only cure was to refuse to allow my gaze to be drawn away, but even then it was more a matter of refusing to worry about the putter than of looking at the ball. It would have been the same if the hole or the line had been drawing my attention. There is nothing more necessary for good putting than to make two entirely separate operations of deciding upon the line and of striking the ball. It is best always to have the first job out of the way so that the entire attention can be given to the second.

CHAPTER FIVE

1   COMMON SENSE AND SHORT SHOTS   71

2   MECHANICS OF THE PITCH   72

3   THE NATURE OF BACKSPIN   74

4   WHAT DISTINGUISHES THE CHIP   75

5   CHOOSING THE CLUB TO FIT THE SHOT   76

6   AN ESSENTIAL FOR SHORT SHOTS   78

7   THE PROPER PROCEDURE JUST OFF THE GREEN   79

Halfway Down

CHAPTER FIVE

I COMMON SENSE AND SHORT SHOTS

Once I was playing with a man who was scoring in the high nineties; yet, to give a sample of his play, on each of two holes, five hundred yards in length, his second shot stopped within forty yards of the green. When anyone who has played golf for any time at all scores much above ninety, the reason can be found in his work around the greens. Of course, older men, who cannot get the needed distance, and the wild fellows, who knock the ball entirely off the course from every tee, are exceptions. Most of the others who play regularly manage somehow to get the ball within short pitching distance of the greens in two shots. It is only then that they really begin to throw away strokes.

An important part of the short play is judgment; selecting the right club and the right shot. Many unnecessary losses are incurred because the player attempts shots that are too exacting—pitching too close to bunkers, and trying to chip cleanly from sand. Not content with a fair average result, too often he will try something that he has not one chance in a hundred of bringing off.

The short shots ought logically to be the easiest to play; in fact they are, if the player can only keep relaxed. The mechanics are simpler, and the effort considerably less; but the closer one gets to the green, or to the hole, the more difficult it becomes to keep on swinging the club. Those who have no trouble lashing out at a full drive with a fine free swing tighten up in every muscle when confronting a pitch of twenty yards.

In playing a pitch, chip, or shot from a bunker near the green, there is one significant difference to be noted between the method of the expert player and that of the duffer; in one case, the swing is amply long, smooth, and unhurried; in the other, it is short and jerky, because the club has not been swung back far enough.

It is a mistake to attempt a steep pitch with backspin when there is ample room for a normal shot. The more spectacular shot may be more exhilarating when it comes off, but the average result will not be so good. Every added requirement of timing, control, and precision will tell in the long run against consistently good performance.

It is demonstrably more difficult to control a shot with a club of extreme loft than with one of moderate pitch. Therefore, the clubs of extreme loft should be left in the bag until the need for them becomes well defined. Nevertheless, whenever it becomes necessary to pitch over a bunker or other hazard, the lofted club must come into play. It is always safer to play a normal shot with a club of adequate loft than to get fancy with a club with a straighter face. But the player who always pitches up to the hole might as well have a hazard in front of him all the time; he does not know how to take advantage of his better position.

There were two circumstances that would induce me to haul a nine-iron out of the bag for use from a lie in the fairway. One was the necessity for pitching over a bunker or other obstruction, when I could not stop the shot with any other club played in a normal manner; the other was a heavy lie from which I knew the ball would take a lot of roll, no matter what I did to it.

Of course, the lie is always a circumstance of importance when one is deciding how much roll to expect. The proper order of procedure is to visualize the shot, to determine where the pitch should drop and how much roll it should have; then to select the club and attempt the shot that should produce this result. Always favor a straightforward shot, and go to a more lofted club only when the necessity for stopping the ball makes this necessary.

2   MECHANICS OF THE PITCH

The pitching stroke, even for the shortest distances, should never be attempted with the wrists and hands alone, nor even with the arms in conjunction with these two. Proportionate to the length of the shot, the turning of the body and shoulders and the use of the legs should be the same as in any other stroke. Indeed, it is my feeling that it is, if anything, more important here than elsewhere, to swing the club head. The swing should be leisurely, of ample length, and with a perceptible crispness as the ball is struck.

The very short pitch, usually made necessary because of the necessity for dropping the ball just over an intervening bunker, is one of the hardest shots for the ordinary player to master. Because of the delicacy required and the high degree of accuracy needed for success, this kind of shot, it seems, results in complete disaster more often than any other. In failing to acquire some proficiency in this department, a player sacrifices one of the greatest stroke savers he could have at his command. Nearly every green on a well-designed course is guarded on the sides by bunkers, so that whenever an approach misses the green by enough to escape the guarding hazards, one of those short pitches is left to play.

I think the most common fault among those who fail with this shot is crouching over the ball. The shot is so small and the player appreciates so well the delicacy of the situation that his first desire is to take every precaution possible. Approaching the shot in this cautious frame of mind, it is not unnatural that he should grip the club short and stoop over as close to the ball as possible, with exactly the same intentions as if a short putt had to be holed.

The best players play this little pitch while standing almost as erectly as they do when playing a full five-iron shot. One notable feature in the method of all is that, even in so short and gentle a stroke, the left arm is fairly straight. The shorter club requires some bend of the body at the waist, but this is, in a measure, offset by the fact that the ball is played much nearer the feet than is the case with the longer irons.

For these little pitches, I can recommend nothing better than a long, leisurely stroke, with the face of the club laid off slightly, and the attempt being made—I hope successfully—to nip sharply at the very bottom of the ball as it rests upon the turf. When it comes off, it is the loveliest shot in the game.

3   THE NATURE OF BACKSPIN

It is a common belief that in playing a backspin shot with a short-iron, the club must be swung in a way that will permit the face of the club head to go through entirely open—that is, looking skyward. Another way of expressing the same thought is that the back of the left hand should be upward. The supposed object of such instruction was to prevent any roll or turn of the wrists, a notion which was thought to produce overspin and a break from right to left in the flight of the ball.

Truly, an open club face at impact produces a slicing spin, and an accentuated roll of the wrists usually results in a hook. But it has been demonstrated, to my satisfaction at least, that neither the hook nor the slice has anything whatever to do with backspin. Jock Hutchison, I suppose, was able to stop almost any kind of shot more quickly than any man living. I watched him several times bring his ball backward five and six feet with a fierce spin that was amazing. Yet Jock always favored a perceptible draw upon every shot to the green. Hutchison could give all proof necessary that a hooking shot may still carry backspin.

Backspin is not sidespin, and it is not obtained by drawing the club face across the ball. The spin that causes the ball to stop is the natural result of contact with a lofted club. If the club had no loft—that is, if its face were vertical—every bit of the force of the blow would be directed toward the center of the ball, and no spin would be imparted.

But an eight-iron has about forty-five degrees of loft, and when it strikes the ball, even in a perfectly normal way, a goodly portion of its force is exerted along the circumference of the ball, and so starts it spinning. The maximum spin would, of course, be imparted by a club of 180 degrees loft, which would to the fullest extent cut the feet from under the ball. The eight-iron is a compromise that impels the ball forward, as it gives it backspin.

The difficulty with the open face idea is that in attempting to carry it out there is danger of taking the ball on the upward arc of the stroke. The face of the club then is moving in a path more nearly at right angles to the plane of its face, and begins to approximate the hypothetical club with no loft at all. Instead of a crisp, firm punch into the ground—a stroke which will produce spin—the shot becomes merely a lob wholly beyond control.

It has helped me a lot to gain this conception of a short-iron pitch. Placing dependence upon the loft of the club, and realizing that I myself was not obliged to do it all, added much on the side of confidence. The chief considerations are a clean contact between club and ball, and a good firm hit.

I am sure every golfer at one time or another has been surprised by a half-topped short-iron that is brought up quickly on the green, stopped by a powerful backspin. This, of course, is the extreme case, where the club meets the ball a descending blow just below center. A greater proportion of the force is exerted on the circumference, and hence a more vicious spin is produced. A lower trajectory accounts for the difference in range.

4   WHAT DISTINGUISHES THE CHIP

For years I provided myself with a run-up club, an old-fashioned cleek with a short shaft, that was to all intents and purposes a lofted putter. I began to use this club for all chipping and run-up shots, and always attempted to swing the club exactly as I was in the habit of swinging a putter; but I found in time a number of reasons why a chip shot cannot be regarded and played as an extended putt.

In the first place, almost all important putting takes place within a radius of forty feet from the hole, and this usually over a keen green, where delicacy and meticulous accuracy are needed. For this reason, a light, sensitive grip must be cultivated, and in the position of address considerations of accuracy must be allowed to prevail over the accommodation of extended motion. In other words, the putting style and grip are developed to suit best the shorter ranges, rather than to facilitate a stroke from the outermost edges of the green. The player naturally handles his putter more easily within forty feet than from outside this limit.

The element of backspin is sometimes important in chipping. It is occasionally desired to play the shot with a slight dragging spin in order to limit the roll of the ball. This, of course, cannot be accomplished by the gentle, sweeping stroke of the putter but must be effected by a longer, more crisply delivered blow. The club must be held in a more capable grip, and the posture must be such that unlimited movement can be accommodated easily.

It is difficult to say when a chip outgrows its classification and becomes a run-up or a pitch; there is no sharp dividing line where one leaves off and the other begins; but there is a very definite separation of putting from anything else in the game; and the player will do well to observe the distinction. He may consider, if he likes, that in chipping he is merely reducing the iron stroke to miniature, but let him not attempt to extend his putting to embrace anything else.

5   CHOOSING THE CLUB TO FIT THE SHOT

A range of shots that twenty years ago had to be played with one club and three variations of method are now played with three clubs and no variation; and it has been found to be a far simpler matter to change a club than a swing.

The value of these additional clubs has been readily appreciated by the average golfer in his play through the green. He no longer needs, and no longer attempts, to shorten the range of a club by cutting the shot or shortening the swing except within very narrow limits. He has a club for almost every distance and, in the long game, he uses them.

Nevertheless, it has been my observation that a further possible simplification on the mechanical side has been neglected, for it is not generally recognized that the wider assortment of implements can be helpful in the short game as well. Just as the varying lofts can be made to take care of the different ranges with little alteration in the swing, so they can also be useful in adjusting the relation of pitch to roll in the very short approaches, without the need for the clever little cuts and delicate backspin shots that introduce so much difficulty.

This is so obviously bad that it sounds foolish; yet it is amazing how many players attempt to play every kind of chip or short approach with one club. You probably know the man well who, as soon as he sees his ball near the green, straightway hauls from his bag some sort of sawed-off five-iron or three-iron. He has already made up his mind to use that club because he has always done so, and he will use it no matter what kind of lie he may have or where the hole may be cut.

Some sort of cleek or run-up club with a short shaft and little loft can be very useful from just off the edge of the green; a club of much loft is uncertain in such a case. The shot to be played is very close to a putt, with only the necessity for lofting the ball over a foot or two of longer grass. But as the ball moves away from the edge of the green and the hole comes closer to that edge, the shot becomes an entirely different proposition.

Except in unusual circumstances, it is always better to pitch to the edge of the green, over the intervening area, which is never so smooth as the putting surface, and it is also better to play every such shot with the same straightforward stroke, without attempting any sort of cut or backspin. This, of course, can almost always be done by changing to a more and more lofted club as the pitch becomes longer and the roll shorter.

I used anything from a three-iron to a nine-iron for shots that could properly be called chip shots. Often when playing to a keen downhill slope, it will be surer to pitch with a nine-iron over even a few feet of intervening space than to run the ball through it; and it is always simpler and safer to play a normal shot with a lofted club, allowing for a normal roll, than to attempt a backspin shot with a club of less loft.

6   AN ESSENTIAL FOR SHORT SHOTS

B illy Burke said that he deemed it important in playing chip
shots to be certain to swing the club back far enough. The
former Open champion cited his own experience and declared that
in starting a round he tried to make certain of an ample backswing
when making his first few chips; after he had struck the first two
or three correctly he knew he could go on doing so.

There are at least two lessons in these words of Bill's. The first,
the long backswing, is always timely, particularly when golfers
begin to talk of overswinging, and of the greater accuracy to be
obtained from a more compact style; the second, equally important, stresses the importance in golf of getting off on the right
foot.

I might say that the first lesson particularly appealed to me because it embodied my own pet idea that most of our short shots—
pitches, chips, and whatnots—are spoiled by a backswing that is
not long enough. The temptation as we near the hole is always to
make the backswing too short and too fast, with the result that all
rhythm and control vanish. In my opinion there has been entirely
too much attention given to the conception that the length of the
shot must be regulated by the length of the backswing, an idea
advanced in an effort to insist upon always retaining the crisp,
decisive quality of the hit. Every shot should be firmly struck; the
importance of this must not be overlooked; but in striving to
assure it we must not be led to the absurd conclusion that we must
come from a hundred yards down to fifty simply by cutting the
backswing in half and swinging with the same force as before.

As a matter of fact, I doubt if it would be possible to notice
any great difference in length between the swing an expert would
use for a pitch of a hundred yards and the one he would employ
for a shot of sixty yards. The chief difference is that in playing
the shorter shot he expends less effort. The contact is kept crisp
and clean but the acceleration becomes more gradual. The ample

backswing certainly is more pleasing to the eye, and it overcomes to a great extent any tendency to hurry the stroke. We all know how difficult it is to play the little shots smoothly and without yielding to the temptation to look up before the ball starts on its way.

The whole idea, it seems to me, is to encourage the player to swing the club head; the longer backswing gives him a feeling of freedom and ease that extends even to his state of mind, and relieves a good bit of his anxiety over the success of the stroke.

7   THE PROPER PROCEDURE JUST OFF THE GREEN

There is a greater variety in the short approach than in any other department of the game. To play these shots consistently well requires more experience and judgment than is called for anywhere else on a golf course. A drive is nearly always a drive, and a five-iron shot, just a five-iron shot. But a chip may be anything, and it rarely is the same thing twice. Especially over keen greens, a man must be a good judge of slopes, and the speed of putting surfaces; he must also be keenly appreciative of the effect upon the roll of the ball to be had from the lie of the ball, the loft of the club, and the trajectory of its brief flight.

The two most important rules to observe are, first, to pitch over the intervening fairway or rough onto the putting surface whenever possible; and, second, to play a straightforward shot without backspin wherever possible. In other words, when sizing up the shot, let the player ask himself a few questions in this order:

"Is there room between the edge of the green and the flag for me to pitch to the green with a normal shot?"

"If so, with what club?"

"If not, can I pitch to the green with backspin and stop the ball quickly enough?"

"If I can, will that shot be more risky than running the ball with a straight-faced club over the intervening ground?"

Of course, all these questions are more easily put than answered correctly. Experience means everything, for every factor —ground, wind, slope, lie—everything must be accounted for and valued accurately.

If the first question is answered in the affirmative, the club selected should be the one to allow a pitch to the edge of the green. Always, one should avoid a quick stopping shot except when it is absolutely necessary. Better results will be had by playing the shot in the simplest way possible. Backspin on such a short shot is very difficult to control. It is almost always better to pitch short of the putting surface or to run the ball across the intervening space, unless it be rough, than to attempt anything unusual or spectacular.

It is also best to keep the trajectory of the ball as flat and allow for as much run as possible under the conditions and in keeping with what I have said above. Often the turf even on the putting surface is not uniform, and a steeper shot is more likely to be affected by irregularities on the surface or by variations in firmness.

Since it is beyond all reasonable expectations that a person may hole a chip shot, little will be gained by playing always for the hole. Naturally, if the ball can be rolled to the edge of the hole, the putt will be simpler whatever the condition of the green, but there are times when a four-foot putt uphill is a far less annoying proposition than one of half that length across a keen slope. It is well to keep in mind that the success of the chip depends upon the success of the putt and is not measured by the number of inches separating the ball from the hole.

CHAPTER SIX

1   GETTING CONTROL   83

2   A LIGHT GRIP   84

3   LOOKING AT THE BALL   85

4   NEVER IMITATE   87

5   THE PENDULUM STROKE   88

6   METHOD   89

7   PUTTING PRACTICE   91

8   MAKING CONTACT   92

9   SHORT PUTTS   94

10 STROKE OR TAP?   96

11 APPROACH PUTTING   97

12 SPOTTING THE LINE   98

13 CHOOSING A PUTTER   100

14 ATTITUDE   101

Maximum Speed

CHAPTER SIX

I GETTING CONTROL

Putting—a game within a game—might justly be said to be the most important part of golf. In almost every championship, or even in friendly matches, if the competitors are anything like evenly matched, the man who will win will be the one enjoying a definite superiority on and around the greens; for it is usually only in finishing a hole that a clear stroke can be picked up. Among first-class competitors, it is hardly ever possible to gain enough in the long game to offset the least bit of loss in putting.

Although much success on the greens may be the subject of moods and luck, I found a few things that happened to cause my moods and luck to be more uniform; particularly helpful did I find them at times when opportunities for practice were not plentiful. Since I regard this as a crucial test, I think they must be good.

The most helpful single thing I was ever able to do to my putting style concerns the left elbow. I found that by bending over enough to produce a decided crook in both arms, and by moving my left elbow away from my body until it pointed almost directly toward the hole, I was able to create a condition of relaxation and easy freedom I could get in no other way. Although I should, by that time, have learned how deceitful are the gods of golf, I could not resist the temptation to write that this came very close to being a panacea for all putting ailments.

The reason for the beneficial effect is that this location of the left elbow places the left hand and wrist under perfect control. I liked to make good use of my left hand in putting, but I knew it caused me many unhappy days, because of its tendency to turn over or to pull the club in as I tried to swing it through—a kind of involuntary flinching that can be ruinous. With the elbow out and the left hand gripping the club so that its back is presented squarely to the hole, I found that the tendency to turn or flinch was almost entirely eliminated.

Whatever may be said by the exponents of all-wrist putting, I know that I did better making some use of my arms depending upon the length of the putt; and I believe others will do better in this way also. The position I have described places the left arm, wrist, and hand almost in one plane, and that plane is very nearly vertical, and parallel to the projected line of the putt. I then tried to complete the stroke by causing the left hand to move forward, keeping always in that plane, and never stopping suddenly at the ball.

2   A LIGHT GRIP

I was talking putting one day with Chandler Egan, who, in addition to being one of the keenest students of golf, was also one of the most reliable putters in the game. "My putting is never right," said Egan, "unless I hold the club like this." He had addressed an imaginary ball as he talked, whereupon he punctuated the sentence by kicking the putter out of his hands with a sharp tap of his foot. He was emphasizing the lightness of his grip. There is nothing more important to remember when one runs into a streak of bad putting. When the little ones begin to slip past the hole and the stroke feels a bit uncertain, there comes a great temptation to tighten the grip, shorten the backswing, and try to guide the ball into the hole; the fact that a similar procedure has failed innumerable times seldom prevents our trying it once more. The truth is that a putt can be successfully steered no more than any other golf shot. On the putting green, as elsewhere, the only hope of success lies in a smooth, accurate stroke that permits the club head to swing freely. When we become afraid to trust this swing, we can expect trouble.

A backswing that is too short goes inevitably with a grip that is too tight. No one ever stabs or jabs a putt when the club is

LOOKING AT THE BALL 85

held gently, and the arms and legs are relaxed; but always something goes wrong when he drops down on the club, crouches low over the ball, and hits it sharply, with the idea that he won't give the face of the club a chance to come off the proper alignment.

Another effort, commonly made to cure bad putting, that always fails, is to keep the body immovable. Alex Smith's whimsical admonition to "miss 'em quick" was more than a waggish sally. Becoming too careful, trying too hard to be precise, causes the player to freeze in his address position. More often than not, this has the effect of introducing a tension or stiffness somewhere that makes a smooth stroke impossible.

I liked to begin with Chandler Egan's loose grip and relaxed position; I liked to feel this grip become a little firmer in the three smaller fingers of my left hand as the club started back; and then, to add a little crispness to the stroke, I liked to feel a tiny flick of the right hand as I struck the ball. I know of no better way of describing the mechanics than to say that the left hand controls the path of the stroke, and the alignment of the face, while the right hand supplies the touch—that nice adjustment of speed that rolls a long putt to the edge of the hole.

To avoid freezing, I liked to keep my knees loose and mobile. It is not a matter of putting with body motion, but of keeping the legs and trunk responsive and ready to move if there should be the slightest suggestion that it may be necessary for them to do so. In other words, there should never be any attempt to putt with the wrists alone, or even with the wrists and arms. When making a very short putt, there may be no movement above the hands, but that is only because no such motion is necessary.

3 LOOKING AT THE BALL

Walter Travis, probably the greatest putter the game has ever seen, always said that he visualized the putting stroke as an attempt to drive an imaginary tack into the back of the ball. I tried this conception and long ago found it to be a valuable aid in putting—to keep in mind the exact line upon which the ball should be started toward the hole. It is all very well to select a point between ball and hole over which the ball must pass; but it is impossible to keep such a point in view, and difficult to keep its location in mind while actually making the stroke. But having selected the spot and allowed the eye to follow the line back to the ball, it is not at all difficult to imagine the line continued through the ball until it emerges at a point on its back side. This is where the tack should be driven—a splendid way of simplifying the operation so that the player can give his entire attention to the making of the stroke. I doubt if any really expert players, except in putting, are aware of looking at any particular point on the surface of the ball. They know it is there and are aware of its location, but the habit of looking at it is so firmly rooted that the act requires no conscious direction. Nevertheless, such players will find that if they direct their sight away from the ball to any degree at all, although they will still strike it passably well, a great deal of their former accuracy will be lost.

Whether or not such players are aware of it, an important factor in the nice control to which most of them are accustomed is the accurate sensing of the relationship between the face of the club and the rear side of the ball's surface with which contact is to be made. In making the address, the sight is drawn to this area, to align the club, and to select the point through which the swing is to be directed; and once the club has moved away, it is the back of the ball, the thing that is to be struck, that holds the player's attention.

The expert golfer senses through his hands the location and alignment of the face of the club throughout his entire swing. Before he starts the club back, he has formed through his eye a mental picture of the way he wants to cause the face of his club to make contact with the ball. Naturally then, unless something disturbs him, he is going to look at the thing he intends to hit, and at the point where he intends to strike it. He would be no more likely to look at the front of the ball than he would be to look at his thumb if he were hammering a nail.

For the average golfer, it will probably be helpful, in putting and in playing short approaches, to follow the suggestion of Walter Travis and to pick out a spot on the back of the ball into which to drive the imaginary tack.

4 NEVER IMITATE

In all my writings on golf, as well as in my motion pictures, the one thing I have tried to stress most is the necessity for assuming a comfortable position before making every shot. There are peculiarities of stance and address that tend to produce certain results; of course, these have to be watched after the player has progressed, but in the beginning I think it is safest simply to stand before the ball in a position that is so comfortable that it is easy to remain relaxed. This, to the beginner, is far more important than any worry about the exact location of the right or left foot.

What I have said is of paramount importance in putting, and in the short game, and I think there is no one who has had a more convincing experience than have I. Up until 1921, my putting was about as bad as one could imagine; I had experimented with it for years, but most of my experiments had taken the form of attempted imitations of some of the good putters I had seen, notable among whom were Walter Travis and Walter Hagen. I had studied the styles of these men, particularly that of Hagen, and would always try to assume the same posture at address, and attempt to swing the putter in the same way. The result of these efforts—and it was a result that should have been expected—was a tension throughout my whole body that would not otherwise have been present, so that however accurately I might reproduce the stroke that had been successful for the man I was imitating, the effect of it was destroyed because I could never relax. After all these experiences, I determined to putt naturally.

The putting stroke is the simplest of all because it is the shortest; once a person has developed a fairly good sense of what it is all about, and once he has developed a rhythmic stroke that can be counted upon to strike the ball truly, the only thing he should worry about is knocking the ball into the hole.

From day to day, I found that my putting posture changed noticeably. I always employed the same grip; I always stood with my feet fairly close together, with my knees slightly bent. Always, too, I saw to it that my back stroke was ample; but sometimes I felt most comfortable facing directly toward the ball; at other times, perhaps a quarter turn away in either direction. Again, there were times when my confidence was increased by gripping the club a few inches down from the end; at other times I liked to hold it at the very end of the shaft.

There are, of course, good putters among the so-called average golfers who by patience, study, and practice have developed putting methods they follow as they would a ritual; on the other hand, these instances are rare.

Anyone who hopes to reduce putting—or any other department of the game of golf for that matter—to an exact science, is in for a serious disappointment, and will only suffer from the attempt. It is wholly a matter of touch, the ability to gauge a slope accurately, and most important of all, the ability to concentrate on the problem at hand, that of getting the ball into the hole and nothing more. I think more potentially good putters have been ruined by attempting to duplicate another method than by any other single factor; by the time they can place themselves in a position they think resembles the attitude of the other man, they find themselves so cramped and strained that a smooth, rhythmic stroke is impossible.

5 THE PENDULUM STROKE

There is one thing I wish people would stop talking about and writing about, because I think it causes much confusion in a beginner's mind. I refer to the theory of the pendulum putting stroke. It has been described and expressed in different ways, but when boiled down, each demonstration resolves itself into a thing absolutely impossible of accomplishment so long as human beings are built as we know them.

Unquestionably, a pendulum-like golf club with an absolutely true face, swung precisely along the line of the putt and suspended from a point exactly over the ball, furnishes the ideal conception of accurate striking. But so long as human toes stick out in front, and until a golf club turns into a croquet mallet and can be swung backward between the legs, there is little hope that this can be attained. For the present at least, it seems to me far better that we strive to find some way to improve our performance, using the method more or less familiar to us all. I have not been converted by my observation of the few players now using putters designed to be swung between the player's feet.

The important considerations in putting are that the putter should be faced properly when it strikes the ball, and that, as it strikes, it should be moving in the direction of the hole. If these two requirements are met, it makes no difference in the world whether or not the club was faced properly or moved along the projected line of the putt throughout the backswing.

6   METHOD

After saying that the correct procedure on the putting green is to decide upon the line and then to concentrate solely upon hitting the ball along that line, it may be helpful to point out a few details of method that will make it easier to swing the club through in this way. As I have often written, to arrange the stance and position too carefully interferes with the freedom of movement so necessary to smooth stroking of the ball; nevertheless, it will pay to arrange certain details correctly.

In the first place, although it is better to stand fairly erect without crouching, one must be careful not to crowd the ball too closely. I am not prepared to say that there is no virtue at all in having the eyes directly above the ball, but I know that more important than anything else is the accomplishment of a smooth, controlled swing. Whenever the player crowds the ball, he makes it difficult for his hands and arms to pass freely back and forth, and necessarily impedes the smoothness of his stroke. He must be far enough from the ball to allow his backswing plenty of room without traveling outside the projected line of his putt.

The second important thing is to keep the ball forward at address so that it can be swept along by a stroke directed along the selected line. As the ball is moved back toward the right foot, the stroke must become more of a hit or jab than a sweep, and therefore must lose in both ease and effectiveness. Only when the ball is addressed approximately off the left toe is it possible to really swing through it toward the hole.

The aim should be to keep the head of the putter relatively close to the ground during both the backswing and the follow-through. I repeat that the correct putting stroke is a sweep, and not a jab or a sharp hit. To accomplish this sort of stroke, it is plain that there must be some movement of the arms both backward and forward.

The putting stroke is in reality the correct golf stroke reduced in scale, especially in the sense that the pull is from the left side. As the stroke comes through, the left arm simply must move forward; if it tightens against the stroke, the putt cannot be truly struck.

The last important point concerns body movement. There is danger in trying consciously to produce a movement of the body in putting, but by all means there should be no attempt to hold the body immovable. A complete relaxation throughout will encourage a quick and easy response to any suggestion of the necessity for movement. Obviously, as the putt becomes longer the hands and arms must have assistance if the stroke is still to be easy and free.

Again, remember: First examine the putt carefully and decide definitely and conclusively the line upon which you want to start the ball. Then think of nothing but hitting the ball along that line.

7 PUTTING PRACTICE

A whole lot of the art of putting depends upon judgment, nerves, a sense of touch, and, as much as anything else, upon luck. But by far the most important part is a sound stroke, by means of which the ball can be struck smoothly and accurately most of the time. Judgment of speed and slope count for very little without the stroke to back it up.

For this reason, there is no finer practice for developing a reliable putting stroke than putting without a hole—just dropping a number of balls on a green or a carpet and stroking them back and forth. Relieved of the need for finding and holding the line, the entire attention can be given to the club and the manner of swinging it.

Now begin swinging and continue with the motion that you are trying to cause the head of the putter to float through the ball. Banish any thought of tapping the ball, sharply or otherwise; in fact, try to forget there is a ball there. Your aim is to swing the head of the putter, and the more freely you can cause it to swing, the better will your job be done.

Strive to make the club swing in a flat arc; that is, to keep it low going back and coming through. Try to swing through the ball, keeping the sole of the putter close to the ground, and direct the swing precisely along the line upon which you intend the ball to start. Above all, let the club swing freely without arriving at any abrupt stopping place.

Forget the silly notion, preached by some, that there is any virtue in half-topping, or up-hitting, or in any other device designed to impart overspin. The fact is that a ball struck with a putter in anything like a normal way will have no spin at all. The contact is not brisk enough to cause the ball to do anything but roll; and you may be sure that it is going to roll where your putter and the slope of the green direct it.

Forget also the idea that it is necessary to keep anything still and fast. Of course, you can move too much, but you won't indulge in gymnastics over a putt of any length, even if you place no restraint upon yourself. You must accomplish the swing approximately as I have described it, and whatever must move, to enable you to do so, should move. You will have to move your hands back with the club to keep the club head low behind the ball; for a very long putt, you may need movement in your shoulders, hips, and legs; your hands will certainly have to move forward to keep the putter traveling close to the ground through the ball. By all means, allow these movements to take place as they are needed. Never should the stroke be allowed to become all hands, all arms, all shoulders, or all anything else. Putting involves a sequence of movements to be performed by the whole of the man, not by any part of him.

If you can learn to swing the club in this way, smoothly and with rhythm, there is nothing that can keep you from becoming a good putter. Once you can have assurance of striking the ball accurately, the ability to appraise slope and speed will not be long in coming. The stroke is the thing.

8   MAKING CONTACT

It is characteristic of the methods of all fine putters that the blade, or head, of the club travels in a very flat arc. In no case does it rise abruptly either on the backswing or after the ball has been struck; but on both sides of the ball, it holds to a course relatively close to the ground. It may be argued that good putting requires a great deal more than accurate striking of the ball, but there is no room for argument that accurate striking is not the first necessity, because it affords the means of translating what the eye sees and the mind directs.

Hitting the ball even ever so slightly on the upstroke is no less a fault on or near the putting green than elsewhere through the fairway. Although it is more difficult to detect in the shorter strokes, there is here the same transference of weight in the stroking action from the right leg to the left that is so noticeable in the long iron play of the better players. Often the even flow forward is not accompanied by a movement that even a high-speed camera could detect, and this has led some to advise that the body should be held motionless in putting. My belief is quite contrary, being, briefly, that complete relaxation and ease of motion is necessary to the accomplishment of a rhythmic stroke of any length, from the shortest putt to the full drive. One cannot start with the intention of making any stroke with the hands alone, or with the arms alone, or with anything else alone, and hope to swing the club easily and with smooth rhythm. The effort to exclude any part or parts of the body from the action, to hold any part motionless, must set up a strain opposing the ease of movement that is so necessary.

In putting, if the club be swung from the left wrist as a hinge, it is obvious that the club head must rise abruptly after striking the ball; obviously, too, it will do the same if the left arm is braced and stopped dead at this point—and, if the blade of the putter should begin to rise a moment too soon, it will be moving upward when it strikes the ball. In order to cause the club head to follow a flatter arc, and to sweep the ball along the proper line, the left wrist must continue its motion. As in every other stroke, better direction and more accurate striking are assured by carrying the left hand on through toward the hole without pulling it in or turning it over. As in every other stroke, there must be no holding back of the weight upon the right leg; the player is not using any particular part or parts of his anatomical structure, he is using it all, and it should all move together.

Whenever I argue this point, I am met with the answer that no photograph of myself discloses any body movement when making a putt of six or eight feet, of the presumably holeable length. I agree that there is no movement that can be measured against a background, but there was, nevertheless—when I was putting well—enough to register upon my own senses. I made no effort to bring about this movement when making a short putt; it was permitted rather than forced, and it was valuable mainly because it gave a comforting assurance of complete re-laxation.

When the rhythm of the stroke became difficult to catch, I

found that it helped to increase the bend at the knees, and at the waist, and to lower the left shoulder when addressing the ball. In this way, the fixing of the weight upon the right leg was effectively discouraged, so that it became easier to sweep the club head through close to the ground.

9 SHORT PUTTS

To miss a putt of a yard length seems the most useless thing in the world. The texture of most of our greens upon which competitions are played is such that no valid excuse is offered the player. In almost every case, one may have assurance that, if struck properly, the ball will find the bottom of the cup.

The short putt presents a problem, because if we allow for the roll of the green, the stroke must be so delicate and the blow so gentle. To strike a crisp, firm, and at the same time gentle blow requires the very ultimate degree of what we call touch, and firm hitting is the essence of good putting.

On a keen green, putts of a yard can be terrifying, especially in medal or stroke competition. The player always has the choice of striking firmly for the back of the cup if he does not like the delicate curling attempt—but then he must think of the putt he might have coming back if he should miss the first.

The mental attitude in which we approach a short putt has a lot to do with our success. When we walk up to a putt of ten or fifteen feet, we are usually intent upon holing it; we know we shan't feel badly if we miss, so our entire attention is devoted to the problem of getting the ball into the hole. But it is quite different when the putt is only a yard long. Then we know that we ought to hole it easily, and yet we cannot fail to recognize the possibility of a miss. Instead of being determined to put the ball into the hole, we become consumed with the fear of failing to do so. Our determination, if we may call it such, is negative. We are trying not to miss the putt rather than to hole it.

A good many short putts are missed because of rank carelessness; the thing looks so simple that it is hard to view it seriously. Yet it will be observed that comparatively few very short putts are missed in the course of a friendly informal round. This would argue that tension and anxiety cause more misses than lack of care, and we might be convinced of this were it not for the diabolical perversity every golfer knows to be inherent in a golf ball. A casual tap with the back of the putter is enough to hole any short putt when no one cares whether it goes in or not, but once large issues are placed upon the result, two hands and a world of pains are required to steer the ball into the hole.

There is nothing so demoralizing as missing a short putt. Many times have I seen a man's entire game, from tee to green, destroyed in the course of a few holes as the result of one little putt. One missed, the next one looks doubly hard; that cast away, too, then the approach putts begin to stop all distances from the cup, applying the pressure with ever greater force; soon putting becomes impossible, and the player begins to force his long game, trying to place his second shots so close to the hole that he will have to do little putting. A rapid progression through these stages before long can result in utter rout.

I do not need to recount the matches in important championships that have been turned by the missing of a tiny putt. Every man who has played golf knows how quickly the tide may turn on such a thing; for the miss not only destroys the player's confidence, it also inspires his opponent.

Long ago I learned that no putt is short enough to take for granted. I have long since recognized the folly of one-handed, backhanded, and all other kinds of disgusted efforts. When it mattered at all whether or not the next stroke went in, no matter how short the putt might have been, it received from me as close attention as I was able to give. I always took a stance and address, even when the ball was lying at the very edge of the hole.

I shall never forget my feeling as I prepared to hole my last putt at Scioto, in Columbus, Ohio, to win the United States Open in 1926. The thing could not have been over three inches in length. Yet, as I stepped up to tap it in, the wildest thought struck me. "What if I should stub my putter into the turf and

fail to move the ball?" I very carefully addressed the putt with
my putter blade off the turf and half-topped the ball into the
hole. Sounds a bit psycho, doesn't it? But golfers can get that
way.

10   STROKE OR TAP?

Luck plays such an important part in putting that a high
degree of consistency, even as high as in the other departments of the game, is virtually impossible. The best putter in the
world can putt miserably on occasions, and the worst can go like
a fiend. The only test is over a stretch long enough to level
out the high and low spots for which luck is to be held ac-
countable.

With this reservation, I think it is possible to generalize to the
extent of saying that the swinger is normally better on the long
approach putts, while the hitter, if he is good, is likely to excel
in holing out from distances of fifteen feet and less. The long,
sweeping stroke that floats the club against the ball is the stroke
for touch and range. When the problem is to bowl the ball great
distances across a keen green and ease it gently up to the holeside,
you can bet, for the long run, on the man who swings his putter
freely.

Although a good touch on the longer putts means considerably
less holing out to do, the man who excels at the shorter distances,
on the other hand, can afford to leave his ball a little farther from
the hole. The short, sharp hit is not the stroke for touch, but
those who use it properly can take up the slack by knocking in
the four-, five-, and six-footers.

The chief difficulty is always in doing the job smoothly, without yanking or jabbing the putt off line. It seems that this is one
of the important arguments in favor of a longer, more leisurely
stroke in which the club head is allowed to do most of the work.
Paul Runyan and Billy Burke hit their putts sharply, after a short
backswing, but they nevertheless swing back smoothly and without hurry. This in itself is something of an achievement the
average golfer will find none too easy.

Stepping up to a putt with the determination to swing helps to relax all the muscles, it encourages smooth action, and discourages any tendency to jab. I think it is decidedly the best method for the greater percentage of players. But here, as in any other place, it is dangerous to ride two horses. Nothing can be worse than to swing back for a gentle, floating stroke and then to yank the club through. If ever you find that you simply must hit, it is best to adopt that method and try to learn to control it.

11 APPROACH PUTTING

Someone wants to know why it is that so many long putts finish short of the hole. This certainly does seem to be a common failing among average golfers. It can be caused, of course, by several different things, among which are inaccurate striking, faulty judgment of the speed of the green, and plain timidity.

The putts that stop a few feet short can very often be laid to the fact that the player has misjudged the speed of the putting surface, for it is quite possible to strike the ball truly and well and still leave it short of the hole; but I do not believe that this is the real reason for the considerable number of long putts that go only a little more than half the desired distance.

My own experience has been that when I was consistently five or six feet short with the big putts, the fault was not in the stroke itself—that is, in the length of the backswing or the power of the stroke—but rather in the application of the blade of the putter to the ball. I mean, to be blunt about it, that I usually was striking the ball a bit above center—half-topping it, in a word; for it is painfully easy to top, or half-top a putt, the smallest of golf shots, whereas a good player very rarely commits this crime with any of the other strokes.

Now, the partially topped putt, where the ball is struck just a shade above the center, is due to one of two causes—hurrying the stroke, or lifting the head too soon. I know that in my case, and I think in most others, the long putt is the one stroke on which it is easiest to look up too soon, and further, to make this vital mistake without being aware of it. Many times I went for days wondering what was the matter with my putting, and never finding out until someone told me that I appeared to be lifting my head too soon. At last I reached a point where this was the first thing I looked for when my putting went off.

But there is one fault in the stroke itself that may produce a tendency to half-top the long putts; this is to be found in the action of the left hand and wrist. A great many golfers, some of fair ability, appear convinced that the putting stroke is so much the business of the hands and wrists that they cannot bring themselves to allow the left hand and arm to swing easily through the small arc required by a putt of even moderate length. Any abrupt stopping of the left hand and wrist must cause the putter blade to come up sharply as the ball is being struck, with a consequent "nipping" of the stroke. Since the putter will not then pass smoothly through the ball, the putt must fail.

It might be said that the best cure for this is simply not to do it. But in order to provide something definite to work on, I might suggest that the right forearm resting lightly against the watch pocket of the trousers makes a fine anchor for the backstroke, not actually immovable, but very nearly so, as far as the body is concerned. Then, as the club is swung through, do not attempt to restrain either arm, but permit the momentum of the club to carry through the ball toward the hole—and let it swing both arms along with it.

12   SPOTTING THE LINE

Certainly, I lay no claim to having reduced the art of putting to anything approaching a science in which there is no variation from day to day, but I found my average performance on the putting green to be greatly improved by following a few principles, none of which has to do with form or the details of the stroke. The first one is to resist the inclination to look up to the hole while in the act of striking the ball, an inclination that becomes stronger when one's putting becomes uncertain. Other players have devised for themselves ways of guarding against this tendency. It makes little difference how long the head is kept down so long as one makes certain that the ball has actually been struck before the eye leaves it.

Absolute concentration upon the ball is materially aided by substituting for the objective of the putt, instead of the hole itself, a spot on the green somewhere along the intended line. For a putt of six to ten or twelve feet—of the length one would normally at least hope to hole—the spot selected should be about halfway to the hole; for a putt of more than this length, the spot should be no more than fifteen feet from the ball. It should then be the player's aim to strike the ball so that it will roll directly over this spot, and he should forget the hole entirely except insofar as his mental picture of the length of the putt will affect the force of his blow. In order to become more consistent, the player should make up his mind to concentrate every effort upon striking the ball truly. If he succeeds here, he cannot go far wrong.

Many good putters will declare that they putt well because they follow through straight toward the hole. Whether or not the follow-through is a virtue, it certainly cannot be a prime cause, for when it takes place, the ball has started on its way. I have never been a believer in a fixed putting style. It has always been my idea that more attention should be given to gauging the effect of a slope, and to estimating the speed of a green—in other words, to training the eye—than to the mechanical perfection of the stroke. It is evident that no matter how accurately the ball may be struck, it must be started on the right line and at the right speed.

As an indication that the line is the important thing, I can truthfully say that I have holed very few putts when I could not see definitely the path the ball should follow into the hole. Sometimes this line seemed to be as clearly defined as if someone had marked it out with white paint; I cannot remember failing at least to hit the hole when I have been able to see the line this clearly.

There is one thing a golfer should always remember and always practice. In any round there are always numbers of times when the proper line to the hole is obscure; if it were always visible, we should miss few putts. But it is always a good practice, when the correct line cannot be determined, to borrow generously from any slope and to attempt to cause the ball to pass a tiny bit above the hole. If the ball remains above the hole, there is always a chance that it will fall into the upper side, and it is certain that it will at any rate stop not far away. But once a putt begins to roll below the hole, every inch it travels carries it farther from that precious cup.

The art of appraising slope and speed—that is, of reading a green—can be derived only from experience. The player who sees only the greens on his home course is at some disadvantage because he comes to know these in spite of himself. In order to broaden his experience, he should play other courses as often as possible.

13   CHOOSING A PUTTER

Nine times out of ten, a change from one type of putter to another will effect no lasting good. The new one may work better at first or on occasions, but consistency would be better served by sticking to the old one and making friends with it.

It is, of course, up to the individual to choose the kind of putter he wants. The design makes little difference so long as the balance is good, the club is easily handled, and the face is true. Whether the head be of aluminum, wood, or iron is a matter of little consequence, generally speaking, although it has been the experience of most good putters that certain kinds of clubs are more reliable under certain conditions.

For instance, the iron putter of medium weight seems to be more effective on fast, keen greens, for with it the ball may be struck more firmly. For the same reason, it is more reliable on putts of ten feet or less. This type is certainly the most popular today in America where greens are small, and very long approach putts are rare. (Remember this was originally written more than thirty years ago—but the principles are still the same.)

Putters of aluminum are splendid implements for rolling a long putt up close to the hole; hence the putt always runs freely and easily over the green. This is a splendid feature when the surface is rough or heavily grassed and slow. These putters are treacherous, however, on very short putts because it is difficult to hit with them both firmly and gently.

The center-shaft putter is usually of an upright lie. It is amazingly effective from short distances. When the ball lies two yards or less from the hole, it is comparatively easy to keep the putter swinging on line with the hole. But this upright position is sometimes embarrassing to a free swing for a long approach putt. It is this difficulty, I believe, that has been largely responsible for the almost complete disappearance of the Schenectady and Travis models.

14 ATTITUDE

Someone told me a story about an experienced professional who regained his putting confidence by rather drastic measures in the middle of a round. Playing well otherwise, he suddenly lost all ability to hole a short putt. After missing several, he was left, at one hole, with a mean one of about four feet. This time he walked quickly up to the ball, closed his eyes, and rapped the recalcitrant sphere straight into the middle of the cup. He holed the next one or two in the normal way and thereafter pursued his way rejoicing.

I should neither attempt nor recommend the method employed here, but there can be no question that anxiety and too much care cause most short putts to go astray. When you see a man obviously trying to guide the short putt, or hitting quickly with a short, stabbing stroke, even though he may hole a few, it will not be long before he meets trouble. A short putt, even as a long one, must be struck with a smooth, unhurried, and confident

stroke. The best way to accomplish this is to decide upon a line
to the hole and to determine to hit the ball on that line and let it
go hang if it wants to. I have never had any better advice in
golf, from tee to green, than was contained in a telegram sent me
by Stewart Maiden in 1919. It read: "Hit 'em hard. They'll land
somewhere." You must not apply this advice literally to putting,
but its application is obvious. Hit the putt as well as you can,
and do not allow worry over the outcome to spoil the stroke.

It is worthy of observation that nearly everyone finds it easier
to stroke properly putts of twelve to fifteen feet than those from
less or greater distances. There is a very good reason why this
should be true. The player fears he will miss a shorter putt, and
fears he may fail to lay a longer one dead, but when he is putting
from the middle distances, he merely hopes he may hole out, without feeling that he must guide the ball into the hole—and he
knows that he will not likely take three putts.

We would all profit greatly if we could cultivate this attitude
toward putts of all lengths; it ought to be easy, too, for we all
know, or should know by this time, that worry does very little
good. If we must be wrong, we may as well make our mistakes
gracefully by choosing the wrong line as by allowing a nervous,
overcareful stroke to pull the ball off direction.

I remember back in my high school days, I was living within
the range of a good iron shot from the East Lake course, and
on nights when the moon was out, I used to go over to the club,
and putt, with a friend and neighbor, on the practice green near
the tenth tee. The moonlight, of course, revealed the hole, and
it also made visible the more prominent slopes and undulations,
but it kindly left obscured the more subtle slopes and irregularities—wormcasts and the like. In this half-revealing light, it was a
source of wonderment to my friend and me that we invariably
putted better than in broad daylight, especially when it came to
holing out from distances up to eight or ten feet.

There must be something to be learned from that moonlight
putting. I believe it to be this—the men who putt well on greens
good and bad must have schooled themselves to see a putting
green as we used to see it in the moonlight.

Let me say here that I do not believe any man can be so accurate in striking a golf ball, or so uncannily precise in his judg-

ment of speed, borrow, roll, and all the other things that go to make a perfect putt, that he can propel a golf ball over ten yards of uneven turf with such unerring certainty that it will find a spot the size of the hole. There are so many factors to be taken into account that the skill required is simply beyond me.

I wonder how many putts that are holed follow exactly the path laid out for them in the player's mind. I should say that as many of those that go down deviate from that path as follow it. It appears to me that the good putter is simply the man who can keep coming close—who gets more times within one-foot radius —and that such a man holes more putts because of the greater number that come close, a greater number more likely will go in.

Working on this idea, it must appear that we should concern ourselves mainly with the more general contours of a slope rather than to try to account for every little hop or roll the ball is likely to take. This does not mean that we should be taking a haphazard shot at the hole, but only that we should determine upon a line upon which we want the ball to start and hit firmly upon that line.

Worrying about rough spots in the green has no effect except to make the stroke indecisive, and I believe that bad putting is due more to the effect the green has upon the player than to that it has upon the action of the ball.

T. W. Palmer, of Miami, was one of the best putters I have ever seen. His theory was that no matter how rough the surface or how bristly the grass, there was always a way to hit the ball so that it would run truly. It really mattered little whether or not he was right or if he could hit the ball in that way so long as he thought he could.

Alex Smith was once asked why he never troubled to remove wormcasts from the line of his putt, his interrogator pointing out that the obstructions might deflect his ball from the hole. "Aye, and they might bounce it into the cup, too," replied Alex.

CHAPTER SEVEN

1   FINDING THE ORTHODOX   107

2   STARTING A NEW SEASON   108

3   THE STRAIGHT LEFT ARM   110

4   USING THE GROUND   113

5   STAYING DOWN TO THE BALL   116

6   TIMING   117

7   DELAYING THE HIT   119

8   CLOSED FACE VS. OPEN FACE   121

9   HITTING FROM THE INSIDE   123

A Short Iron

CHAPTER SEVEN

I FINDING THE ORTHODOX

Golfing methods differ from each other in many particulars. Each good player presents an appearance so unlike any other that he can be recognized from great distances merely by the manner in which he swings the club. The inexperienced observer often fastens onto these differences, concludes that each man employs a radically different swing, and sets about modeling his form upon that of a player he will select; this one he will ape faithfully and exactly to the last detail.

A closer study of the better players reveals that although no two are alike, or even nearly so, still there are certain things that all do. Not only are we justified in regarding these unanimously accepted practices as sound, but it would seem that every golfer, large or small, fat or lean, would do well to adopt them as his own. The fact that almost every effective swing displays certain things in common with all others is evidence enough that these things ought to be parts of every method. Indeed, these are about the only details of the stroke the instructor is able to give to a rank beginner; these are the only things that he can tell him positively to do. The rest of the teacher's job is to correct faulty movements and to fit together a stroke upon the proper foundation already supplied; but the stroke as a whole is not developed upon any set lines. Fundamentals must be observed, but much latitude is allowed for accommodating individual needs.

A thorough understanding of the fundamentals of the stroke should be the first aim of the beginner. It may be said, of course, that there is a fundamentally correct swing from which everyone should vary only slightly. But that is not what I mean, for a thorough understanding of this sort of swing, and the ability to produce it, are the two things that all of us have been seeking and so few have ever attained. I have reference only to the obvious things that are easily seen and accomplished by the average inexperienced player, things that an ordinarily good player learns for himself, and an expert never has to think about. Nevertheless, these points can be noted by everyone to his advantage.

One reason for the consistency of the best players is the possession of a sound swing; meaning nothing more than a swing in which the successive positions are taken in accordance with accepted practice among expert players. It will be found that the man who departs far from what we call the orthodox, even if he is at times effective, is yet an erratic and unreliable player. He who starts in an unexciting position, and commits no unwarranted extravagance, is usually the more consistent player, because he places himself in positions and moves his club in paths from which, and through which, other successful players have found the going easier. All men are enough alike to make it safe to follow examples proved effective by others.

2   STARTING A NEW SEASON

The most trying time of the year for the golfer is always the time when he comes out of hibernation and begins to tune his game back to a point where he can again enjoy it. After a long winter layoff, each club feels like a broom handle, and each ball when struck transmits a shock up the shaft, causing the player to think he has hit a lump of iron. Golf is not much fun during this period; but it is a period we must endure to enjoy the pleasures beyond.

Any man would be grateful, I think, for any hints that might help him get through this "tuning up" period with as little suffering as possible. Although all of us do not have the same troubles and need to apply the same correctives, when we are playing regularly, I noticed that my companions manifested much the same tendencies when suffering from lack of practice. Apparently, golfing muscles lose much in elasticity and responsiveness when not in use, and being unaccustomed to performing normal functions, act upon demand in much the same way for all individuals.

The first failure is in the length of the backswing; it is not hard to detect in any case a tendency to shorten the backward motion, and to whip the club back to the ball almost before it has reached the shoulder position. This is one way in which lack of assurance is manifested, the player being actually afraid to let himself out as far as he would if extended to midsummer form.

The second failing in part results from the first, although it is also attributable to the fact that the winter layoff has impaired the sense of timing. This sense is entirely dependent upon practice, and when one fails to practice, or play, he must lose the rhythm of the stroke. But it will be noted that in the spring the error is always on the fast side; no one ever swings too slowly.

The third common tendency is to attempt to lift the ball instead of striking it firmly downward. This, I think, is due to a slack left hand and wrist. The player is not quite certain that he has done everything correctly, so that he reaches the ball with the feeling that he perhaps ought to turn back to try it over again. Then he either slackens his grip or pulls the punch and spoils the shot.

These are not all the sorrows that may be encountered during the first few rounds of spring, but they are those most commonly experienced. If we could start out on the lookout for them and promptly put them away, our days in purgatory would be lessened considerably. Let us resolve, then, that in the coming spring we will swing back slowly, that we will swing back far enough—even farther than we think necessary—that we will grip firmly with the left hand, and that we will punch briskly through the ball. If we will do, and remember, these few things, it will not be long before we find the groove.

My own experience each year was somewhat tantalizing. From the end of the Amateur Championship until warm weather came again, I usually played only three or four rounds, sometimes with as much as two months intervening between successive attempts. On these occasions, I went out relaxed and with very little concern about the results I might be able to obtain. Then I played fairly well. But when spring drew near, and I began to play a bit more often, I found myself doing the very things I have mentioned above. The first round, when nothing much was expected, was not so bad, but after that the trouble began.

3   THE STRAIGHT LEFT ARM

Good form in any physical activity must be valued in terms of efficiency. The efficiency of a thermal engine, for example, is measured by the ratio of the work done by the engine to the heat energy supplied to it. The efficiency of a golf stroke must be measured, in the same way, by the ratio of the work done on the ball to the amount of physical energy used up in the swinging. The expert golfer drives far with little apparent effort because of the high rate of efficiency of his performance. The duffer, though he strain himself to the utmost, falls far behind because so much of the energy expended goes to waste.

A high rate of efficiency, and hence good form, in golf, depends upon three things: the development of the greatest possible club head speed at contact, with whatever energy or power the player can supply; the achievement of a precisely accurate contact between club and ball, directing the blow along the line upon which it is intended that the ball shall travel; and consistency in performing approximately according to these standards.

Although these are obvious generalities, it is helpful to do a little thinking along these lines in order to appreciate the importance to a golfer of a proper use of his left arm. For it is in this particular that all duffers are most appallingly deficient, and here, too, that the better players most often go astray.

For some persons, a straight left arm is a physical impossibility. So let us say that an extended left arm is one of the prime requisites of good form. In many ways, it contributes to club head speed, accurate contact, and consistency of performance—the three components of the efficiency rate.

Just now we are interested chiefly in the backswing. The backward movement is merely the means of storing up power to be used in the hitting—but to increase the amount of this stored-up energy is of first importance. We have seen that the beginning was made in the hips in order to assure that the windup of the body would at least be started. When this had progressed a short distance, we began to force the club back with the left arm.

Now with the club having completed about half of its backward travel, the left arm has become almost straight, and is pushing the club as far back as it can comfortably go. The arc of the swing is thus made wide so that the space and time for adding speed to the club head coming down will be as great as possible.

The player who allows his left arm to bend perceptibly is sacrificing width of arc and power. His swing, because it is not as wide as it could be, is that much away from the ideal of efficiency that he could make it.

There is nothing in the straight left arm that, of itself, increases the power of the swing. It is a part of a sound method, for those who are able to keep it straight, because it is the factor which definitely limits the arc of the backswing. Consequently, when the arm is straight, this arc is as wide as it can be made, and the swing can then be more easily repeated time after time in the same groove. Except that the bending of the arm reduces the width of the arc, and hence the time and space within which the speed of the club head may be built up, the chief loss from the bend is in precision.

At that, few players keep the left arm rigidly straight during the backswing. I like to have the feeling of pushing the club back with the left arm because this assures that it will be reasonably extended, but the arm does not become completely straight until it is stretched out by the beginning of the reverse turn of the hips, back toward the ball, while the club is completing its backward movement.

In order to complete a backswing of full length, at the same time keeping the left arm even approximately straight, there must be a good bit of movement in the hips and waist. Naturally, a good free turn of the hips is not so easy for the player past middle age, whose waistline lacks some of the suppleness of former years. If he wants to get the club back at all, the left elbow simply must give a little. There is no other way.

The important thing, so far as the left arm is concerned, is that it should not collapse in the act of hitting. In the motion pictures of Harry Vardon, made when the great Englishman had passed his sixtieth birthday, a bend of almost ninety degrees could be seen in the left elbow at the top of the swing. Yet as soon as the hip-turn had stretched out the left side, this arm became straight, and remained so until after the ball had been struck. The bend at the top, then, is by no means fatal if the succeeding movements are performed correctly.

What will help most is complete relaxation. Timing and rhythm can make up a lot in power. By all means, swing the club freely, both backward and forward, and avoid the tightening a short backswing must produce.

But now that we are able to say what the left arm should do, we are up against the far more difficult problem of finding a way to make it do what it ought to. It is easy enough to say, "Keep the left arm straight." But the average golfer wants to know how he can do it.

Briefly stated, I think the most common cause of the collapse of the left arm in the act of striking results from the left elbow, in one way or another, being forced in against the side of the body. Many players seem to fear that the club head will not catch up in time. Consequently, they attempt to throw, or "cowtail" it in ahead of the hands—exactly the thing that causes the left arm to fold up and become entirely useless. I have seen a good instructor, upon taking charge of such a pupil, shock him almost out of his senses by telling him to try to hit the ball with the sole of his club. The only thing intended to be accomplished by such advice was to turn the left elbow away from the side, so that the left arm could carry through.

An examination of the grips used by expert golfers will show that in every instance the left hand is to some degree on top of the shaft. The effect of this is to present the elbow somewhat toward the hole, and to prevent a clamping of the upper left arm against the side of the body. The left arm should work closely across the chest and front, but there must never be any suggestion of the player's "hugging himself" with it.

4   USING THE GROUND

No matter how simple the correct golf stroke ought to be, the job of describing it in language everyone can understand is not so easy. Those of us who strive to do this are continually searching for new ways of saying the same thing, in the hope that some new slant will appeal to those who have missed the older one. Since, in the last analysis, it is a feel we are trying to impart, even the most accurate exposition of the successive movements often finds the pupil entirely unresponsive. What he needs is the inspiration from some phrase or idea that will enable him to get the feel for himself.

One such phrase, of comparatively recent origin, I like very much. Now one hears quite often of a player "using the ground" in hitting a golf ball. There is nothing new in the meaning it is intended to convey, but it is a different way of presenting the old idea, and I have no doubt that it will strike many players with more force than anything previously said to them.

The average golfer is most deficient in his body movement. In the first stage, he is inclined to swing the club entirely with the arms. In the next stage, yielding to persuasion, he begins to make some use of the upper portion of his body. But sometimes one begins to think that nothing will ever bring him to the point where he will make sufficient use of his legs and hips— in other words, "use the ground."

Somewhere Abe Mitchell wrote that the player should "move freely beneath himself." To me, this is an excellent way of suggesting the ample use of legs and hips underneath a head that maintains an approximately fixed location to act as anchor for the swing. It suggests both the lateral and turning hip-movement characteristic of the better players. But I think "using the ground" adds something to this.

The idea of "using the ground" does away first with the notion that the feet must be rooted firmly and fixedly in the turf. It implies, of course, a positive connection, but the conception is one of action rather than of being solidly planted. The player who intends to use his legs is not so likely to put them out of commission by "statuizing" himself before he begins his swing.

A tremendous amount of power can be derived from a correct use of the hips, legs, and the muscles of the back. These sources are almost entirely neglected by the average golfer, who swings the club mainly with his arms. In the correct swing, the left hip leads the movement back toward the ball, generating speed and power as the unwinding progresses. At the instant of impact, the hips have turned through their positions at address, and the lower part of the body is facing almost squarely toward the hole. The unwinding of the hips culminates in a sort of wrench just before the club meets the ball, both legs combining to produce a sudden and powerful thrust up the left side of the body.

It so happens that I feel and control this movement in the hips. But there is no reason why it should not be sensed and controlled through the feet. The turn of the body, of course, would not be feasible unless the feet maintained a positive grip upon the ground. The feeling of giving the ground a wrench with the feet may be easier for some than the sense of compelling the hip movement in some other way.

"Using the ground" means using the hips and legs. The man who stands flat upon both feet throughout the swing and moves his club by means of his arms and shoulders is not doing either. Neither is he making much of a golf swing. Whether one prefers to "swing beneath himself" or "use the ground," he must get some use from his legs in order to play good golf.

Starting with both toes turned slightly outward, a great many players make the mistake of raising the left heel at the very start of the backswing by bending the left knee directly over the left foot without any semblance of a turn. The effect of this action quite obviously is to cause too much weight to remain on the left foot at the top of the swing, in addition to effecting a serious restriction of the turn away from the ball.

It is possible to describe the correct backward turn as a movement of the hips or of the knees or of the feet. All have their parts to do, but it is not likely that all players would derive an equally clear conception if the thing were treated in only one way.

As related to the feet, then, the correct action transfers the weight supported by the left leg to the inside of the foot, and at the top of the swing the left heel has been pulled from the ground and the inside of the ball of the foot is bearing the burden. The exact reverse of this action takes place on the right side, for there the weight at the top of the swing rests upon the outside of the heel. In my own case, and in that of all players who employ a full body turn, the weight is moved so far back on the right foot that the large toe is actually lifted from the ground.

To think of starting the backward motion by moving the weight over to the inside of the ball of the left foot is often the easiest way to originate the correct action, for this movement of itself turns the left knee back and forces the turn of the right side. Of course, the same result could be accomplished by thinking of the movement of the knee itself or of the turn of the hips. It is purely a question of the easiest method for the individual.

It is important, whatever method is followed, that the motion be smooth and unhurried. In order that it may be so, there must be no precarious position at address from which a hurried takeoff would be likely—an easy, comfortable position, with the weight borne about equally by the two feet and resting neither upon the heel nor the toe of either foot.

Two things sadly neglected by the average golfer are footwork and body movement. They begin, as it were, at the wrong end of the problem, working first upon the control of the club head by the arms, and then turning the body or moving the feet and knees just enough to accommodate the necessary travel of the arms. The golf swing is, of course, a thing to be done by arms and body, but I do not believe that the body motion should be limited by the arm movement. An English surgeon points out that the trunk muscles are the most powerful muscles of the body, and, although I do not agree with the methods he recommends for their use, yet he is eminently right when he says that they ought to be used actively.

In fact, there can be little question that the turn of the hips and shoulders, and the accommodation and balancing of this turn upon the feet and legs is the essence of effective form. In the accomplishment of it is found the most noticeable difference between the expert and the handicap man. It is largely responsible for the difference between 240 yards and the 175 which the arm-swinger is happy to attain.

5   STAYING DOWN TO THE BALL

The average golfer would be a lot better off if no one had ever said anything about the necessity for keeping the eyes glued upon the ball. There is infinite virtue, as so many have pointed out, in maintaining some sort of anchor for the swing. I always think of it as "staying down to the ball." But when a person begins to think about keeping his head immovable and concentrates upon keeping his eye fixed upon the ball, trouble is being invited. The very act of trying to do something that is natural to do anyway sets up a tension that is hard to break. It is perfectly natural to look at an object one is trying to hit, and ordinary observation and awareness of its presence and location are sufficient. When a man gazes fixedly at a golf ball, he is doing something wholly unnecessary and destructive of the rhythm and relaxation he has striven for. I have found little value in the maxim, "keep your eye on the ball," except on the putting green and in playing very short approaches. The longer shots that are missed are usually caused by something else.

Although it is unquestionably true that, in order to strike the ball accurately, the player's eye must correctly observe the point of contact, still it is a fact that there can be faults in the swing which may cause the head to come up without having any relation to a desire to see too quickly where the ball may be going. So many times, the average golfer accuses himself of looking up when he is lifting his head for quite a different reason.

It is true that on the putting green, the ultimate objective, the hole, and several intermediate ones, in the succession of little spots which constitute the line are so tantalizingly near to the player's field of vision as he addresses the ball that some effort is required to assure concentration upon the one important act of striking the ball correctly. For this reason, it often helps to fix the gaze consciously upon a point on the ball's surface which it is intended shall be struck.

But this difficulty does not exist when a drive from the tee or a long shot to the green is to be made. In such cases, it is

comparatively easy to detach oneself from distant objects sufficiently to give attention to the ball. And then one rarely looks
up. It is the most natural thing in the world, when distractions
have been removed, to look at the thing that is to be struck, and
the possibility becomes very remote that the player will lift his
head too soon if he swings his club correctly. The expert player
hardly ever tops a brassie shot, not because of the determined
way in which he keeps his eye glued upon the ball, but because
his correct swing allows him to keep his head down.

The correct swing is performed by the entire body under a
head that is practically stationary. Some have called the head
the anchor of the swing, and perhaps that is as sound a conception as could be found. The important thing is that the chin
does not, and must not, turn around with the shoulders, but on
the contrary, actually moves toward the rear as the swing sweeps
forward beneath it.

The most common cause of head lifting is to be found in
the right side. Whenever the right side and right arm, instead
of holding the player down, fail in this function and produce
a sort of heaving stroke, the head is forced to move. When this
is recognized, we can go back still farther and fix the fault mainly
upon a too-early discharge of the cock of the wrists. When this
angle straightens out too early in the downstroke, the club head
is forced below its proper path, and the heave becomes necessary
in order to bring it up to the ball.

The player who preserves the angle of his wrist-cock, and who
keeps his swing down by means of the proper action of the
right side, and a taut left arm, does not need to worry about
looking up. Indeed, he will find nothing in the world so interesting, at this particular moment, as the back side of the ball
that he is going to strike.

6   TIMING

It is unfortunate that the most important feature of the golf
stroke is so difficult to explain or to understand. We all talk
about good timing, and faulty timing, and the importance of

timing, and yet no one has been able to fix upon a means of saying what timing is. The duffer is told that he spoils his shot because his stroke is not properly timed, but no one can tell him how he can time it properly.

One common error causing bad timing can be pointed out with sufficient exactness to give the enterprising average golfer something to work on. I mean the error of beginning to hit too early in the downward stroke. I have said that it is a common error. It is an error common to all golfers, a chronic lapse in the case of the expert, but an unfailing habit in the case of the dub. I believe it will be found that of the players who turn in scores of ninety and over, ninety-nine out of every hundred hit too soon on ninety-nine out of every hundred strokes. Many who play even better golf and have really acceptable form fail to play better than they do for this very reason.

Hitting too soon is a fault of timing in itself. It causes the player to reach the ball with a large part of the power of the stroke already spent. Instead of being able to apply it all behind the ball, he has expended a vast amount upon the air where it could do no good. Apparently, everyone fears that he will not be able to strike out in time when, as a matter of fact, there has not been one single player come under my observation who has been habitually guilty of late hitting. Sometimes he will fail to close the face of the club by the time the club reaches the ball, but this is always due to something entirely apart from tardy delivery.

The primary cause of early hitting is to be found in the action of the right hand and wrist. If the left hand has a firm grip upon the club, so long as it remains in control there can be no premature hitting. The left side is striking backhanded, and it will prefer to pull from the left shoulder, with the left elbow straight, rather than to deliver a blow involving an uncocking of the wrists.

But the right hand throughout the stroke is in the more powerful position. Its part in the stroke is on what in tennis would be called the forehand. It is moving forward in the direction easiest for it to follow. Because the player is intent upon effort, and upon hitting hard, the right hand tends to get into the fight long before it has any right to enter. The right hand must be restrained if it is not to hit before its time arrives.

7   DELAYING THE HIT

I wish everyone could study carefully a few sets of motion pictures showing the proper action of the right side, noting particularly the successive positions of the wrists. In the case of an expert player, the wrists remain fully cocked, just as they were at the top of the swing, until at least half of the down-stroke has been completed by the arms.

The dub, on the other hand, starts immediately when coming down to whip the club with his wrists. He forthwith takes all the coil out of his spring, and when his hands reach the position corresponding to the numeral eight on the dial of a watch, his wrists are perfectly straight, and all the power left is in his arms and shoulders, to be utilized by any twist or contortion the player can execute.

Whenever you see a player (who is apparently going along easily) blow wide open under the strain of competition, the chances are that the most immediate cause of the detonation is an unruly right hand, a hand that has gotten out of control because of the anxiety and nervousness of the player.

I think I can say truthfully that I am always on guard against a misapplication of right-hand power, but that even then it gets me. For a right-handed person it is, of course, perfectly natural to want to do everything with that hand, and it becomes necessary not to call it in when it is needed, but to keep it out when it is not. The consciousness is of exclusion rather than of use. To my mind, the right hand is absolutely useless, except as a steady-ing factor, throughout the entire backswing, and nearly half of the downstroke, or hitting stroke. Its first real use comes when it assumes command for the actual delivery of the blow.

If we allow the right hand to take hold at the very beginning of the downstroke, we are hitting too soon. The swing has not a chance to get started in the right groove, and the power is apt to be spent too soon; the wrists will have been uncocked before the stored-up energy can be expended upon the ball.

Of course, so long as we swing a golf club with two hands, in order to swing it properly, both hands must be used correctly. But with most players the effort must be to subdue the right at certain important stages, rather than to direct it to positive activity. It has been said that the correct swing is a wholly artificial, unnatural procedure. In the sense that a naturally right-handed person must force the left side and discourage the right, this is certainly true.

This alone is sufficient reason for stressing the left side most strongly; since it must be used, and yet it is unnatural to use it, it requires more conscious direction than the right. A right-handed person, swinging a right-handed golf club, will not need to think about hitting with his right hand; he will need only to make certain that he does not begin to use it too soon, or incorrectly. On the other hand, if he does not think about moving his left side, it will surely get in the way, and gum things up.

My conception of the correct swing is built around the one thought of making the left side move, both in taking the club back and in swinging it through. This is the main idea. The use of the right hand, though important, is yet a subheading. It has to be thought of only in order to keep it from overpowering the left, and asserting itself in a disastrous way.

The correct backswing originates with a turn of the body away from the ball, a movement which is controlled and actuated by the left side; as the body movement begins to pull the hands away, the left arm begins to push the club back. The average golfer, swinging the club in what for him is a natural way, picks it up with his right hand. Immediately, his club goes up over his shoulders. The left side, left arm, and the all-important windup of the hips are forgotten. The hips fail to turn because there is nothing to force, or even to encourage, them to do so. The lifting action, started in this way, can be continued almost indefinitely without the aid of the body turn.

It is important to avoid this pickup with the right hand at the beginning of the backswing. This is one time when the right hand should do nothing but maintain an easy grip on the club, and respond to and assist lightly the movement of the left. If it does move, it will almost certainly cause trouble.

8   CLOSED FACE VS. OPEN FACE

For the last decade, golfers have talked and written much about the merits of the "open-face" style of play as compared, or opposed, to that which they designate as the "shut-face" method. All of us are familiar with these expressions; but I am quite certain that there is no general understanding of the details of the two strokes that would enable a person to make an intelligent choice between the two. In fact, I fear that the closed, or shut-face has been so generally discredited as a difficult and unreliable variation that few care to consider that it may have advantages; but some of the best players in the world, including two who have never been surpassed for brilliance when in the proper mood, deserve to be classed as exponents of the shut-face.

I do not know who originated this means of distinguishing between the two methods, although I think it is as good as can be found. It is generally understood that the face of the club is open when, at the top of the swing, its toe points directly toward the ground; and that it is closed when, at the same stage, the face is looking skyward, and the length of the blade is horizontal. Of course, these are only the more obvious characteristics of the two methods that result from other more important differences. My friend, Elliot Cockell of London, an earnest student of the game, remarked, most pertinently, that he was never able to detect the least difference between the open- and the shut-face club at the instant the ball was being struck. The reason he has not discovered such a difference is that is does not exist. The difference lies solely in the series of motions necessary to bring the club to the top, either open or closed, and in the second series necessary to bring it from its position at the top to the ball, in proper alignment. Actually, to hit the ball while the club face is either open or closed would bring disaster; by this time, the open face must have closed sufficiently, and the closed face

opened enough, to cause each to meet the ball squared to the
line of flight.

I considered Leo Diegel and Jess Sweetser the two leaders
among those who employed the so-called shut-face method; and
I think that because the play of each could be paralleled so closely
—that is, their strong points and weaknesses were so nearly the
same—as to provide good evidence that errors were inherent in
the method in the hands of the very best. I do not mean to say
that either was noticeably weak in any department, but merely
that both did some things better than they did others.

I think I remarked after playing a practice round at Hoylake
with Diegel that there was no man living who could keep putting
long shots as close to the flag as could Diegel, on his day; on
second thought, I amended that by adding—except Jess Sweetser.
That day at Hoylake, Leo started home 3, 2, 3, 2, all birdies on
holes requiring shots to the green of from 140 to 190 yards; and
each one kept going closer and closer until the last one, on the
thirteenth, we could not ask him to putt. On another day at
Brookline, Massachusetts, in 1922, while he was giving me an
artistic beating in the National Amateur, I saw Jess Sweetser go
out in 32 without holing even a fair putt. He holed a full
pitch at the second hole, and hit two more pins in the nine
holes. Sweetser's spade-mashie had always been as accurate as a
Springfield rifle, and just as comforting to the enemy.

Apparently then, the shut-face method, causing the club head
to travel longer on the line of play, and for a greater space
looking at the ball, is admirably suited to accurate iron play.
Neither Diegel nor Sweetser was an exceptional wood club player;
that is, although both were good enough in this department, the
driving of each was somewhat off the superlative excellence of
his work with the irons. Diegel was an unusually long driver,
but both he and Sweetser, if they went off at all, were inclined
to err with the wood. I think that this is also characteristic of
the shut-face method, which does not seem to be well adapted
to the sweeping stroke of the full drive.

A closer study of the shut-face style reveals a definite difference between it and the open-face method from the very moment when the backswing commences. I think that a reliable
conception of this difference can be had by producing a mental

picture of the action of the shoulders in each type of swing.
The open-face player, in taking the club back, executes a
simple rotation of his upper body around the spine as an axis;
since this axis will be tipped forward a bit in the act of addressing
the ball, the shoulders will move in a plane only slightly inclined from the horizontal; meanwhile, the left hand will turn
a bit over the right. On the other hand, the shut-face player
forces his left shoulder quite low on the backswing, so that his
left hand will be shoved under the right. Said another way, in
the early stages of the backswing, the open-face player will tend
to pronate his left hand, the shut-face player to supinate his.

Again, when the shut-face swing nears the hitting area, there
is a perceptible difference, for in order to open the face before
impact, this time the right shoulder must go under. In each
instance, in the cases of Sweetser and Diegel, there is a rolling
of the shoulders forward and backward that is not seen in the
swings of those who open the face of the club.

9 HITTING FROM THE INSIDE

Our knowledge of the various movements making up the swing
of an expert player is at best indefinite, especially when one
tries to apply and adapt his general observations to his own game.
Photography has made it possible for us to see with sufficient
exactness what actually takes place when an expert hits a golf
ball, but we are as much in the dark as ever when we try to
reproduce what we have observed. The player cannot see himself.
He, therefore, must play and adjust his stroke wholly by feel,
and unfortunately no two sensibilities react in precisely the same
way to like influences.

I thought of this one year at Augusta just before the Southeast-
ern Open. Mr. Alexander Revell was telling of taking lessons from
Johnny McDermott and of McDermott's advice to swing the club
through the ball outward toward the right edge of the fairway.

Mr. Revell stated that in his case the attempt to do this nearly always resulted in a straight drive.

J. Douglas Edgar was the first man I remember to have enunciated the doctrine of the inside-out swing, although apparently McDermott had used the idea before. Edgar even devised what he called a "gateway" through which he made his pupils swing. I am not certain that his lessons with it were always successful, for I know numbers of his pupils in Atlanta who religiously followed him, and nearly all of them were chronic hookers.

I have always thought that the ideal stroke propelled the club through the ball directly on the line of flight. I cannot conceive that a straight shot could be hit in any other way. Necessarily, the club cannot follow this imaginary line for any great distance, but it is only important that it do so during the time it is in contact with the ball, while the club head is traveling less than an inch.

Methods differ in detail among individuals, but the mechanical requirements of a perfect drive do not vary. As Mr. Revell obtained good results by attempting to swing out toward the right edge of the fairway, so I, at Minikahda in 1927, managed to drive well employing exactly opposite tactics. All during the National Amateur Championship of that year, I was resisting a tendency to hook, evidently caused by hitting the ball too briskly from the inside. My straight shots resulted when I attempted to swing my hands toward the left edge of the fairway.

In any event, the straight shot is accomplished by the straight hit. But the individual plays by "feel." In applying the principle of correction by exaggeration, by trying to swing in one direction, he merely avoids swinging in another. In other words, by trying to hit from the inside, the player really does no more than avoid hitting from the outside.

CHAPTER EIGHT

1   POWER   127

2   DRIVING FOR DISTANCE   129

3   HITTING HARD   133

4   FAIRWAY WOODS   135

Swinging Through the Ball

CHAPTER EIGHT

I   POWER

There are more than a few golfers in this land who wonder why, and how it is, that even when they connect sweetly with a drive, it never goes as far as an ordinary shot by a youth of much less physical power. Most of all, it puzzles athletes who still possess brawn and muscle far exceeding that of any first-class golfer in the game today. They cannot understand how a little 120-pound kid can stand up all day long and wallop drives far beyond the very best efforts they could produce in a year.

Physical strength does count for something in golf. It would be foolish to say that it does not, for although we may talk all we please about rhythm, timing, and whatnot, still the man who hits the ball hardest will achieve the longest drive. Rhythm, timing, and the other essentials of form merely determine which player can deliver the hardest blow.

Long driving, up to a certain point, may be explained by good timing. By this I mean that the increased length obtained by the whole rank of first-class players over that obtained by the second-class can be largely attributed to better timing. The dub suffers because he rarely expends his power where it will do the most good. But within the group of players we refer to as first class, there are a few who are able to drive a good bit farther than any of their fellows. This increase, I think, is not explainable on the basis of timing, for all the better players are good in this respect; these extra yards obtainable by the few are traceable to form and not timing.

Every now and then, even the average golfer will meet the ball exactly right—so far as timing and feel are concerned. When he does so, he reaches the ultimate for him; yet a more proficient player of much less physical strength has no difficulty in passing by many yards his longest drive. The things making this possible are to be found in the swing—the increased body turn, the hands high at the top of the backswing, the length and greater fullness of the arc.

The longest hitters in my day were Charles Lacy, Charlie Hall, Cyril Tolley, Bill Stout, and a Frenchman, Marcel Dallemagne. A noticeable feature of the style of each was a fast pivot or hip turn as the club approached the ball coming down. They made the best use of the most powerful muscles of the body, those of the back and hips, and by doing so, they gained over the rest of the field those few extra yards that made them stand out.

The average golfer uses his hips and body very little. He takes the club back mainly with his arms and he hits without making any great effort with the muscles of his back. The player who is a little better, but still not expert, turns more; he may even turn back quite nicely, but an observer will note that his turn into a ball is retarded—he may even stop his pivot before he hits the ball. The expert employs a full turn, and continues his turn forward uninterrupted through the hitting area—and the very long driver whips his hips around like a flash.

Almost every first-class golfer turns his hips quite freely away from the ball during the backswing. In nearly every case, the back of the player will be presented squarely to the hole—that is, the upper part of the back between the shoulders, for necessarily the hips turn less than the upper portions. There is a noticeable amount of twisting above the waist.

If this turn and twist are regarded just as the wrist-cock, as a source of power the problem is then to unwind in proper timing to deliver the maximum blow at the right instant. The expert golfer begins to unwind his hips at the beginning of his downswing. The turn back to the ball begins slowly, just as the downswing itself begins slowly, and the sudden powerful twist is reserved for hitting just as the wrist-cock is saved. It is important that the left hip should turn out of the way, but it is also important that the hips should not be twisted so quickly that the power of their unwinding will be used up in the first part of the downward stroke.

The action of the left knee almost exactly parallels the correct wrist action. This knee bends forward—to the player's front, not toward the hole—and swings to the right during the backswing. During the downstroke, it swings to the left, but does not straighten immediately; it actually becomes straight just before impact as the final powerful twist of the hips takes place. It is this twist that straightens the leg and throws the kneecap back and gives the impression, so often stated, that the player is "hitting against the left leg." I dislike this expression, because it suggests that a resistance is interposed by the left side. It is far better to "hit with the left leg."

As a matter of fact, there is no question that the long hitters twist the hips through quite an arc, and they actually do so with a great deal of effort; I do not know how to describe it better than to say that it is a powerful wrench of the body.

When playing well, I have the feeling that during the first part of the downstroke I am pulling against something. There really is nothing to pull against except the tension in my own muscles— set up by the effort of the stroke. More or less rapidly this is overcome, and finally wrists, body, arms, and legs all join to deliver their power simultaneously. The proper timing of these factors, with each one prepared to the limit, is the real secret of long driving.

2 DRIVING FOR DISTANCE

Years ago, I preferred a driver with very little depth of face, and I had a habit of tossing my ball onto the grass of the tee and driving it from there; but I noticed that in this way my usual shot began low and climbed quite rapidly toward the end of its flight, when it would drop quite lifeless to the ground.

It was quite evident that this trajectory and lack of roll were due to excessive underspin produced by the downward direction of the stroke at impact. Beginning then, I made some experiments with clubs of greater depth of face, teeing the ball well up so that the stroke would not have to be so abruptly downward. I even designed and had built a driver of a face-depth of 1⅞ inches. These experiments convinced me that, whatever might be developed in theory, there was actually more length to be obtained from this combination of deep face and high tee, especially when I made an effort to hit the ball squarely in the back, with the club moving, as nearly as possible, in a direction parallel with the ground. Underspin is a virtue in the play of any approaching shot, whether off an iron or a wood club, because the spin tends to steady the ball in flight, and to control its roll after it strikes the ground. But where extreme length is desired, and the direction does not need to be precise, the aim should be to impart as little underspin as possible.

Some years ago I had the satisfaction of seeing this idea tested upon a driving machine holding an actual golf club. In these tests, the ball was first placed so that it would be struck by the club head a fraction of an inch before it had reached the lowest point of the stroke. Several drives were made from this location, and after these distances were noted, the ball was teed so that the club head would make contact after it had passed the lowest point. All drives from the second position were longer than any from the first. All the while, of course, the machine was swinging the club with the same speed and force.

For my own part, I want no more conclusive demonstration that our aim in driving should be to impart to the ball as little underspin as possible. Of course, the high tee and the deep face are not requisite, for the same stroke can be accomplished with a club of shallow face driving a ball from a lower tee; but the high tee unquestionably makes the stroke easier of accomplishment, and the greater depth of face gives the player confidence. As in everything else, we can overdo ourselves here, as I found with my specially constructed driver. After a certain point, as the depth of the face becomes greater, the use of the club becomes increasingly difficult. This one finally became too much for me. Although I hit with it some of the longest drives of my life, the club was too treacherous with the smaller, heavier ball, and hickory shafts. I might have done quite well with it had I had today's ball and the steel shaft.

A person beginning golf is usually advised to omit the driver from his first kit, for the reason that, until he gains some idea of what it is all about, he will find the brassie, or two-wood, with its greater loft, a far more satisfactory club, even from the tee. This is not bad advice, for like the one-iron, the driver is more difficult to play than its more lofted brothers, the brassie and spoon. It demands a more accurate and more powerful stroke to get the ball into the air and to propel it along a proper line of flight.

I have even heard the opinion expressed that a properly designed driver was practically useless to 80 per cent of the people who play golf, and I have been told that Chick Evans played in at least one National Championship playing all tee shots with a brassie, the only wood club he carries.

The sponsors of the Oregon Open Championship in 1932 saw fit to revive the old custom of having a driving contest in connection with their golf tournament. Some of us can remember when no invitation or sectional tournament was quite complete without its quota of driving, pitching, and putting contests, and consolation flights to furnish excuses for giving away a little more silverware. In this particular instance, however, the Portland people apparently had a very good and a very interesting reason for adding this event to their program. Each contestant drove three times with the new standard ball and three times with the 1931 standard ball, thus affording an opportunity for actual human demonstration of the difference between the two.

The manufacturers and the U.S.G.A. had told us that on a 250-yard drive the new ball was approximately five yards shorter than the old. But that was the figure determined by tests with a driving machine. It is comforting to see that the human experiment arrived at approximately the same result.

Gene Sarazen made the longest drive with the old ball, and tied with two others for top position with the new, his best efforts being 253 yards with the old and 242 with the new. This shows a difference of eleven yards, but a better measure is found in the average of the ten best drives with each ball. These average figures were 236 and 231.2, a difference of only 4.8 yards, within two-tenths of a yard of the approximate difference the officials had noted.

It was possible also to draw another conclusion comforting to the dub—that it is the long hitter who loses most distance by the change. I am sure that we who declared that a difference of five yards in 250 meant less in 175, were not taken very seriously. The Portland driving contest seemed to indicate that this was true; for while the top figures varied eleven yards with the two balls, yet when the distance became less than 230, the difference became smaller, so that the average difference was reduced to less than five yards—not a conclusively accurate demonstration, but a fairly good indication.

One other thing of importance by way of comparing the two balls was shown, and this may be taken as encouraging or not, depending upon whether the individual desires that golf be a test of skill or become as easy as possible. From all that appears in the report, the same number of drives were made with each ball, each player driving three of the old and three of the new. Nineteen of the first finished within the boundaries, while only fifteen of the latter were fair, indicating that the lighter ball is a bit more responsive to inaccuracies of striking.

A driving contest always shows up our exaggerated notions of what constitutes a long drive. It always teaches us that the prodigious distances we read about are either inaccurately guessed at, or are due to hard ground, downhill roll, following wind, or some other unusual circumstance. We read about a lot of drives over three hundred yards, but we are rarely aware of the exact conditions of play. We become so accustomed to figures above 275 that we regard 240 yards as a puny effort for a first-class golfer.

I have seen two driving contests in which really first-class golfers competed. In one at St. Louis in 1921, at the time of the National Amateur Championship, I was myself a competitor. Both were staged on level ground—at St. Louis on a polo field—with no appreciable wind stirring. The only difference lay in the condition of the turf—at St. Louis it was rain-sodden, while at Lytham-St. Anne's in England, a fair roll was obtainable. I myself won the St. Louis event with an average for three drives of 229 yards, and the longest single shot was by Bob Gardner of Chicago, good for 246 yards. The winner of the St. Anne's event —I think it was Archie Compston—averaged less than 250 yards, and the longest drive traveled 263 yards, roll included. In 1932 Sarazen's drive of 253 yards was the longest among a field of good pros.

I have heard that there was in New York an operator of a driving range of three hundred yards of level ground who offered a wager of five thousand dollars that no one could drive the length of it both ways within a time period limited only so as to make it unlikely that he might be driving in both directions with the wind behind. He permitted the taker to pick his day and time. I hope no one took him up without considering that when a yard becomes thirty-six inches of level ground, three hundred of them go a long way.

3   HITTING HARD

The more one sees of golf, the harder it becomes to make anything out of the various theories about how hard or how gently a ball should be struck. We hear that "pressing" is a thing to be avoided; but when we determine to avoid it, the first thing we know, some kind friend will inform us that we are steering the ball, and that we should hit it harder.

Truly, it is a difficult thing to know just what to do. There is unquestionably a world of grief ahead for the man who continually goes all-out after every shot. Extremely hard hitting necessarily involves a considerable sacrifice of control, often with no increase in length, because the ball is not squarely struck; but there is equal danger when the player pulls his punch, easing up the stroke in an effort to guide the ball down the middle of the fairway.

Once I was playing with Phillips Finlay at Pebble Beach. There had been so much talk about Phil's long driving that the publicity given that part of his game must have affected the boy's play. Few people appreciated that his long hitting was due to anything but unadulterated slugging; they could not understand that such distances would be covered by what, for Finlay, was a normal drive. So always when Phil had a bad day with his wood clubs, the criticism was always that he had been pressing.

Whether Phil had been aware of it or not, this sort of thing had its effect upon his game. Whenever he found his drives going off line, the suggestion of critics was the first thing that occurred to him, so that he immediately eased up his stroke in an effort to hit the ball straight. On this day when we played, he had quite a lot of trouble on the first nine, getting a little farther from his normal stride at each tee shot as he held himself back more and more.

Finally, after hitting a half-smothered hook off the ninth tee into the rough, where he lost his ball, he asked me what I thought was the trouble. I replied that he appeared to be holding himself back too much, and that I thought he would do better if he would take a good healthy wallop instead.

He had been hooking steadily up to that time. At the tenth hole, he hit a very long ball, that barely missed the fairway to the right, and fell into the bay. From that point on, he drove very well, indeed.

This does not indicate by any means that slugging should be the order of things. It shows merely that a conception of hitting that will cause the player to hold-up, or to fail to go through with the stroke, is entirely wrong—probably it will cause more trouble than the other in the long run. In driving, it has always been my idea that one should hit as hard as he can without upsetting the balance of the body and the timing of the stroke. Pressing causes trouble mainly by speeding up the backstroke. If that can be made slowly, and the downward stroke started leisurely, there may be any amount of effort thereafter without cause for worry.

4   FAIRWAY WOODS

Without overstepping the bounds of a proper conservatism, it is possible to say that a good part of the average golfer's difficulty comes from the understandable desire and effort to do more than he can, and nowhere is this more noticeable than in his use of the wood clubs through the green. Time after time, he may be seen diving into formidable rough with a spoon in his hand, or hauling out a powerful brassie to dig a ball out of a cuppy lie—shots that a golfer of greater skill and experience would not think of trying. The determination to get length at any cost, to use the strongest club possible, more often than not leads him to exceed his limit. Certainly, the average of his results would be greatly improved if he would make a practice of always using a club with which he could be sure of getting the ball up.

At least part of the trouble comes from a confused idea of the relation between the individual clubs of the present-day four-club set of woods and those of the old driver-brassie-spoon combination. The inexperienced player is always more likely to choose a club because of the number on it than because of what he can do with it.

To be perfectly frank, except for the exceptional case of the man who hits his long shots moderately well and with a fair amount of power but fritters away strokes around the greens, the player who is above the 85 to 90 class has little need for the driver or brassie of the four-club set. In almost every instance, players of this class have trouble getting the ball up, even from the tee, and they would be wise to drive with the two-wood, play their long fairway shots from good lies with the three-wood, and reserve the four-wood for shots of somewhat shorter range or from tight, unfavorable lies.

It must be understood that the conventional four-club set covers approximately the same range of loft as did the conventional three-club set. It is merely divided among four clubs instead of three, in order better to meet the demands of the more accomplished players. Even before this arrangement was made available in matched sets, most of the pros and better amateurs were using four-wood clubs. Some called the additional intermediate club a driving brassie; others inserted it lower down and named it a brassie-spoon. My own set was made up of a driver and brassie, both of somewhat less than conventional loft, a spoon with the same characteristic, and a lofted spoon. I called these last two "big spoon" and "little spoon," respectively.

This, and similar sets put together by other players, were substantially the same as the modern four-club matched set. The brassie, being a bit more powerful than the conventional brassie of that time, was useful in stretching out to reach the long holes in two, when a good lie made this ambition appear reasonable. The big spoon could get good length from less favorable lies, and the little spoon could plant a steep shot upon a green from the shorter ranges. The big spoon, corresponding to the three-wood, could get the ball up more safely and easily, and had very nearly as much range as the ordinary brassie.

It is not possible, of course, to tell a person just what he can or cannot do with a particular club; this he must find out for himself; but he might remember that the three-wood of the average set of today has about as much right to be called a brassie as the two-wood, and is often a safer club to use. When length is desired, it is, of course, best to use a powerful club, but one should always be sure that the club selected is one that will get the ball up easily.

CHAPTER NINE

1   SLICING AND HOOKING   139

2   CAUSE AND EFFECT   141

3   CURING THE SLICE   143

4   THE MAGIC LINE   145

5   "EDUCATING" THE SLICE OR HOOK   147

6   PULLING   149

7   HOOKING   150

8   FADING AND DRAWING   151

9   SHANKING   152

Unwinding the Trunk

CHAPTER NINE

I   SLICING AND HOOKING

It is too bad, in a way, that so many persons are inclined to regard expert golfers as natural phenomena, playing the shot through some sort of instinct that enables them to swing the club subconsciously in the proper groove. Because they are so adept at swinging a club, it is thought, I suppose, that they were born with the knack, and that they never have to use an ounce of gray matter except in selecting clubs. I say that this is too bad. I don't mean that it is too bad that the players are so misunderstood—they can bear this very well—but it is too bad that the average player cannot understand that even the very best pros have constantly to be on guard against the myriad faults that may creep into any swing, and that they all have to know how to correct each one of these faults, and to prevent a recurrence after one has been put down. It is too bad, because the average player ought to realize that he must study his faults, and learn to correct them.

There are two directions in which a golfer may err in any particular stroke. He may be off line to the left or to the right; he may hook or he may slice. If he knows why he hooks, and why he slices, and is able to effect a rough-and-ready remedy, he is in fine shape to hand out a lot of good lacings to those he plays with. But it rarely does any good just to say that hooking or slicing can be corrected by shifting the right hand, or doing some other simple thing; for, although the actual spin that causes slicing or hooking is produced because the club strikes the ball in a certain way, still the fault of the stroke inducing such a contact is not always the same.

Unfortunately, the natural reaction of the player, when he is fearful of either slicing or hooking, always tempts him to do the very thing that will cause him to exaggerate, rather than correct, the fault. Whenever a man standing on a tee suddenly thinks that he must not slice, almost invariably, as he brings his club down to the ball, he will pull his hands in close to his body in an effort to yank the shot over to the left side of the fairway. When he does this, he pulls the face of the club across the ball from the outside even more emphatically than he would have done had he continued his normal stroke.

This much is common knowledge; the slicing spin, and the way in which it is produced, are generally understood among all golfers. But the manner of producing a hooking spin, or what to do to counteract a slice, is not so universally known.

I remember my old friend J. Douglas Edgar used to say that the hooking spin was produced by compressing the inside of the ball—that is, by striking the ball, not directly from the back, but somewhat from the inside out. It is safe to assume that when a player is hooking badly, he is exaggerating this sort of hit; in other words, he is shoving his club out too fast, and probably taking the ball too much on the upstroke. I am, of course, excluding from this discussion the badly smothered shot, speaking only of the hook that gains a fair elevation, and is not merely bounced along the ground.

So the average player has two extremes between which he can work. Let him know that when he is slicing he is cutting across the ball from the outside, and let him try to get his club more around his body on the backswing, so that he will be well behind the line of flight, and thus can have a better chance of striking outward at the ball; and let him know, too, that when he is hooking, he is taking the ball too much from the inside, and that he should endeavor to straighten out the path of his club head within the hitting area, so that it will pass more nearly along the line of flight, and not so much outwardly across it.

To do this, he must watch his left hand and arm, and be certain that the left hand is not throwing the club away from the body. When I have been bothered by hooking, I have always found it helpful to pick out a spot on the left side of the fairway, and to try to swing my left hand through the ball, toward the spot. It is a curious fact that the simplest remedy for slicing or hooking is to try deliberately to hit the ball toward the spot where the slice or the hook usually lands; for, if one tries to neutralize a hook by shoving the shot out to the right, or to correct a slice by pulling the ball over to the left, the only thing accomplished is an exaggeration of the fault sought to be avoided.

Douglas Edgar was a magician with a golf club. When driving along a fence marking a boundary of the course, he preferred to start his ball down the line of the fence, or even outside this line, and bring it back into the fairway by a fade or draw, whichever was needed. He said that if he played for a swing of the ball to either left or right, he knew it would move in that direction; if he tried to hit a straight shot, he could not be sure in which direction the ball might veer.

2 CAUSE AND EFFECT

Two very important things for the average golfer to remember are: First, that it does not help to throw the club head into the ball ahead of the hands; and second, that the right arm should not begin to rotate nor the right wrist begin to turn or climb over the left until after the ball has been struck. To attempt to get the club head in first, or to roll the wrists, are two favorite ways of trying to correct a slice. The only trouble is that neither ever works.

To hit a golf shot correctly, the player must move toward the ball, not away from it, as his club gathers speed. At the instant of contact, he must be over the ball where he can perform consistently and accurately the job of hitting; and above all, he must be in position to utilize the pull of his left side. He cannot expect to get results by standing back and throwing the club at the ball.

The correct stroke causes the club head to approach the ball from inside the line of play. The factors making this possible are the forward shift of the hips during the downstroke, maintaining a bend in the right arm that keeps the right elbow close to the side of the body, and the backhand nature of the stroke dominated by a strong pull from the left side. These are the factors that make it necessary or inevitable that at the instant of impact the hands should be on a line with, or ahead, of the club head, and that the left hand should carry through the ball without beginning to turn.

The immediate cause of a slice is a contact between club and ball while the face of the club is directed to the right of the line upon which the club is moving. These conditions may be met when the club head is moving precisely along the line of intended flight but when it is facing to the right of that line, or when the face is square to the line and the club head is moving across it toward the player's left. Unless the grip of the left hand has been relaxed enough to allow the club to turn in the fingers, the first set of conditions is rarely ever encountered. In correcting a tendency toward slicing, the problem is almost always to correct the direction of motion of the club head.

Instead of making this correction, the attempt to whip the club head in first only leads to more difficulty. The effort to hold everything back to allow the club head to get in front prevents the completion of the forward shift of the hips, and assures that the stroke must cross the line of play from the outside, precisely the thing sought to be avoided.

The better idea is to concentrate upon holding the swing behind the line of flight passing through the ball. It is possible to groove a swing that hits down from the top, but not one that moves the club head outward.

When the weight stays back on the right foot, and the forward shift is not completed, the stroke, as I have said, must come from the outside in. The result of such a stroke depends upon what the hands do to the face of the club. If the right hand rolls over the left before the ball is struck, the result must be a badly hooked or smothered shot; if not, a curving slice, whether or not the ball finishes in the fairway.

In a sound golf stroke, the back of the left hand is visible at the instant of impact to an observer standing in front of the player. It is important that this hand should drive straight through the impact position in the effort to direct the head of the club precisely along the line of play. The turning action, which begins to take place an appreciable space after contact, does so then because the player's muscles relax after the effort of hitting, and because his swing has then reached the limit of motion it can accommodate along the line of flight.

3 CURING THE SLICE

The sliced shot, apart from its directional error, is always very weak, and the person who finds himself always cutting across the ball appears to be about as helpless as a golfer can be. To try to help such a person, I am jotting down a few points that may help him recognize and correct his troubles.

First, let him examine his backswing to see if he turns his hips as far away from the ball as he might do with comfort. The idea here should be to make the swing come well around so that there will be a possibility of staying always well within the projected line of flight; a restricted hip turn in the backswing tends to force the club head into a more upright arc as it is moved by the arms and hands alone.

The hips should begin to turn at the very beginning of the backswing, and every effort should be made to keep the right hand from lifting the club. At the top of the swing, the hands should be approximately above the right shoulder. If the player has swung around to this extent, at least he will have avoided a position that will force him to cut across the ball.

But he still must look out for trouble; there are two mistakes

likely to make their appearance at this point. One results from
an improper handling of the weight of the body. The correct
action from this point involves a forward turn or unwinding of
the hips, starting the downswing, which clears the way for the
right elbow to drop in close to the side, and thus to deliver the
blow from behind the ball. If this movement is not made, and
the weight of the body is held back on the right foot, the swing
must be forced to the outside, and the club must cut across the
ball.

The other mistake, commonly made at the top of the swing,
results when the right hand takes hold of the club in an effort
to hit too quickly. Many players have the notion that they should
start the club down by throwing it with the hands. Those who
do this should throw the club completely away and start over,
for this stroke has been spoiled beyond recall.

Although it is proper to say that the path of the club head
should be controlled by the left arm and side, still it is important
to know what the right hand and arm should be doing all this
while, in order not to offer too much interference. The most difficult action for the beginner to understand is that of the right
arm during the first part of the downstroke; and this action has
a very immediate connection with his tendency to cut across the
ball. The important features of this part of the swing occur to me
somewhat as follows:

First—That the right elbow at the top of the swing should not
come up too far, the best position being one that leaves the upper
part of the arm about parallel with the ground.

Second—That the first movement of the right arm on the
way down should return the right elbow to the side of the body;
and

Third—That the angle between the shaft of the club and the
right forearm should not change during the first part of the
downstroke; in other words, that the right wrist should not
change its angle of cock until the downswing is well under way.
This last assures that the right hand will not take command too
soon.

These are some of the things for the habitual slicer to keep
in mind. Generally, he needs additional freedom in his swing; and

particularly he should strive to get this freedom somewhere in the region around his waist and hips. He needs, above all else, an ample body turn in order to get himself into a position from which his arms will have a chance to function properly.

4   THE MAGIC LINE

One cannot help sympathizing with the poor fellow trying desperately to find some way of building up a sound swing when he finds himself submerged in a sea of "do's" and "don'ts" with scarcely a chance of finding his way out; there can be no question that the chief reason golf is so mystifying to the beginner is the difficulty of expressing, in a few words, the simple, fundamental, necessities of form. There are numbers of players who devote enough thought, time, and hard practice to the game to make them reasonably good golfers if they might start out with an accurate conception of what they want to do; but in so many instances there is a confusion of ideas, making intelligent progress impossible.

One cannot select one movement, or even one series of movements, and say that this, or these, is, or are, fundamental; if a basic principle is to be found, it must be broader than this; it must be an idea, rather than a prescribed procedure that can be charted upon a blackboard; it must be something for the player to accomplish with the club, rather than with his own body.

I lay no claim of invention or discovery to the theory of hitting from the inside out. I don't even know that I agree that such a manner of hitting is indispensable to good golf; but I do believe that the duffer seeking a fundamental conception to guide his practice, and his development, cannot do better than to resolve never to permit his club head to cross the projected line of flight back of the ball. Whether he will cross that line at or after impact depends entirely upon the kind of shot he wants to play.

Almost every inferior player swings across the line of flight from the outside to the inside; he is either a hooker or slicer, depending upon whether the club face is open or closed at impact. One rarely finds a dub who stays at all times inside the magic line.

Suppose we look at the problem in this way: There are two points in the swing to be watched, two places where a misdirected move may make a crossing of the magic line inevitable. One is at the moment when the club is started backward from the ball; the other occurs as the club is started downward from the top. If a man will practice starting upward and starting down with this in mind, I believe he can very soon learn to swing in a proper groove.

In starting the club backward, there is one thing that may throw it outside. This is the right hand. If the player initiates the motion by breaking his wrists, almost inevitably his right hand and wrist will lift the club and carry it upward over his shoulders.

A proper start of the backswing is made by rotating the entire body, by turning the hips and shoulders upon a pivot, at the same time bending the left knee and lifting the left foot from the ground. I can think of no better way to make a start than by "taking off" from the left foot, by rolling the weight toward the inside of that foot. The arms may move slightly, but only a few inches across the body; the hands—moving straight backward —drag the club away from the ball along the line of flight, then turn toward the inside.

This turning and swinging, following naturally, lead to a proper position at the top of the swing, with hands well back and the club pointing over the back of the neck to a point several yards to the right of the objective.

This is the second critical point; at least two things can be done here to throw the club head beyond the line. To start with a pure turn of the body, without moving the hips forward, is fatal because such a motion pulls the hands forward, causing the club head to move toward the player's rear; to swing first outward, then inward and across the ball, is then not only easy but inevitable. The same thing happens if the wrists are employed here to whip the club downward, as is so often advised.

There are three things that must be done at the top to keep

the club swinging inside the line of flight. They are: First, the hips must be shifted quickly toward the front along the line of play, ever so slightly, yet definitely; second, the right elbow must return to the side of the body; and third, the hands must be moved or dropped a few inches backward and downward, without straightening or starting to straighten the wrists. If this sort of start is made, the rest is easy.

I do not believe that the direction of the blow at impact should actually be from the inside out unless the player desires to produce a draw or hook; to play a straight shot, the club should travel along the line of flight; but anything is better than playing always and helplessly across the ball from the outside. Sometimes, to produce a fade or slice, it must be done, but when the player cannot help doing it, he is in a discouraging predicament.

5   "EDUCATING" THE SLICE OR HOOK

In almost every group of golfers, in the habit of playing a lot together, there will be one with the reputation for getting a lot out of a poor game. Usually, the person so maligned, or complimented, whichever way you view it, will be an awkward-looking player who slices or hooks every shot, but who makes allowance for the error, and so manages to keep his ball in the fairway. No one will be foolish enough to consider him a golfer, but the very consistency with which he makes the same error sometimes enables him to return surprisingly low scores.

I think it was Macdonald Smith who once said that he never tried to correct a tendency to hook or slice during a round. The man with the "educated" curve may take consolation from that, but in reality it should afford him none. It is not unusual for an expert player to find, on certain days, that he has more confidence in fading or drawing the ball into the flag than in playing it straight. On such occasions, as Mac Smith said, it is unwise to go contrary to this preference. But the dub actually hooks and slices; the bend he must allow for could not be described as a fade or draw.

When Mac Smith played a shot like this, he knew how he did it and could tell when it was going to happen; to an uncanny degree, he could tell how much curve the ball would take. But the dub allows for the hook or slice only because he has always had it before; he does not know why he has had it, nor how to stop it; above all, he does not know how much he will get, or if he will get it at all.

It happens often that the man who aims far to the left of the fairway, anticipating a decided slice, will bring off a hook of equal proportions. This is the one place in golf where the short player has a definite advantage—he will not have to come back so far.

There have been a number of fine golfers who preferred to play every shot with a fade or draw. J. Douglas Edgar was one of them, and when he was in the mood, he could do wonders with a golf ball. I saw him return a 66 in the last round of the Canadian Open of 1919, and I think he played not one single straight shot in the entire round. He was bending everything in from the right or left, over fences and trees and anything else that happened to be handy. He appeared to pick out the worst trouble, hit his ball straight at it, and then turn it back into the fairway as if it were on a string.

But even a man as capable as Edgar could not play consistently in this way; he had to be touched by some bit of inspiration; at other times, when he was not exactly right, he could score very badly.

So the man who habitually allows for a hook or slice, instead of setting about to correct it, can never hope to do much with his golf. On days when he repeats the fault consistently, he may get along nicely, and really do better than he has any right to expect. But he has not enough control over his swing to enable him to consciously produce the curve; when he does happen to hit one straight, or bend it in the other direction, he will have a good day's work getting back to the fairway where he intended to be playing.

6   PULLING

A pulled shot is one that flies straight, without noticeable curve to right or left, but is merely misdirected to the left of the intended line; a hook is understood to be a shot that may start on any line, but breaks or curves to the left. The alignment of the club face and the direction of its travel at the instant of impact is, of course, not the same in the two cases. A pull, that is, a shot flying on a straight line directed to the left of the objective, results when the club face is approximately square to its direction of motion but at impact is moving across the line of play from the outside in. A hook results when the club is facing to the left of the line upon which it is moving as it strikes the ball. As the contact between club and ball endures for only the tiniest fraction of a second, we do not need to look for extended lines or intervals of time.

Usually a player who hits the ball well enough to score in the high seventies, and particularly one who drives well, might be suspected of exaggerating the inside-out idea, producing his hooked shot by hitting too much to the outside. But the fact that hooks are mixed in equally with pulled shots means that the fault cannot be this. The requirements for hooking can be met with the club traveling across the line of play from either side, or even precisely along that line, but a pull cannot result when the club is crossing from inside-out.

The trouble comes from holding the weight a shade too long upon the right foot, a fault that throws the downswing out beyond its proper path, and results in hitting across the line of play toward the inside, or to the left of the objective. Obviously, the club face must have been completely reclosed by the time it meets the ball, resulting in a straight flight in the direction the club was traveling. When it closes a little more, the hook appears, and if the fault is exaggerated, there is a complete smother.

I should recommend moving the weight at the beginning of

the downswing a little more quickly from the right foot to the left, actually making the first movement in the unwinding of the hips a shift directly toward the objective. Here the right elbow, which has been drawn away from the side of the body in completing the upswing, should return to the ribs in order to keep the arc of the swing inside the line of play. Exert a strong pull from the left side and continue it straight through the ball. Hit the ball slightly downward and visualize a swing straight through toward the objective.

7   HOOKING

Whenever a man who is a fairly good swinger finds himself beset by a fit of hooking, the first suspicion is that he is hitting the ball on the upstroke; in other words, making contact after the club has passed the low point of its arc. Although hooking is definitely a fault of the better player, there is nothing that can make a capable golfer appear or feel more helpless; and in a great majority of cases, he will have to be told what he is doing.

The dub is rarely guilty in this particular, because he has not yet learned to keep his swing inside the line of play. He swings the club back outside this line, and in most instances, cuts across the ball from the outside. He is most commonly a slicer, and when he errs on the other side, the result is usually a pull or bad smother. The shot that gets up into the air well enough, but curves sharply to the left, is the one that has been hit upward.

The hook in this swing results directly from the failure of the left side of the body to carry on through the ball. The usual sequence begins with a bracing of the left leg that locks the left hip and stops its turn; the hip then obstructs the left arm, causing it to collapse in order to complete the swing. In extreme cases, the player may feel himself shoved back upon his right foot as he hits, so that he cannot help striking upward.

The things to watch, obviously, are the left hip, the left

arm, and the cock of the wrists. First, to be sure that the unwinding of the body is led by the left side and that the hips shall not stop their turn too soon; second, that the left arm does not quit, relax, or collapse before the club has passed a safe distance beyond the ball; and, third, that the effect of the wrist-cock is not lost by discharging it too early in the downstroke. A tee shot should not be knocked down when ultimate length is desired, but when it becomes a matter of correcting a destructive hook, it is best to try to hit the ball down in order to keep it in the fairway.

Probably the most difficult thing for the player to believe is that easing off the swing aggravates, rather than corrects, this fault. As soon as we begin to take the thing more quietly, the hip turn begins to stop sooner and the left arm to collapse more completely. We then find ourselves desperately trying to steer the ball down the course. What we want to do instead is to hit hard, and by forcing the swing, to make the hips go around and the left arm to keep going.

8 FADING AND DRAWING

George Trevor wrote quite interestingly of an observation he attributes to Henry Cotton, the brilliant English professional concerning what he claims to be the essential difference between British and American golfing methods. The distinction pointed out by Cotton was that British golfers favor the outside-in swinging arc over the American inside-out, and hence play every shot with a fade as against the Yankee draw. I suppose, if there is one fundamental difference between the styles of play prevalent in the two countries, Cotton has correctly pointed it out.

Yet I do not think that the difference is more than one of preference. Certainly, the top-rank players of either country are able to fade or draw at will and with almost equally good control in either case. When Cotton states his rule, he cannot mean that the ability to play either shot is lacking on either side; he can mean only that in play off the tee and in approaching a green faced squarely to the player when no advantage is to be gained by coming on from either side, the British will choose the left-to-right shot and the American the right-to-left. In this I agree.

I suppose the influence of Vardon and Taylor can be seen in this. But Vardon was an upright swinger, and for an upright swinger, the left-to-right shot is the more natural and, therefore, the easier. About the time when I was coming along, soon after Vardon had made his second visit to this country, the fading shot gained great, if short-lived, popularity because it was said to be more easily controlled. It was admitted to be shorter off the tee, but it was said to bring up more quickly after hitting the ground and, therefore, less likely to roll into trouble from fairway or green.

In America, on the other hand, we learned our early golf from the Scots, who were more or less flat swingers, and they did not teach us to swing like Vardon. The influence of the master, when it began to be felt later, could do little more than induce our later generation to effect a sort of compromise.

I think that Cotton is right in saying that the Yankee draw is a more effective method of hitting a golf ball. The tail end hook, which is not really a hook, but a curl, almost always adds a good many yards to the drive, and it is, for me at any rate, far more satisfactory in playing a long boring iron shot to the green. Further, a familiarity with its use does more than anything else to overcome one of the most troublesome things in golf— a hard crosswind off the left side of the fairway.

9   SHANKING

Although shanking is not the most universal of golfing mistakes, it certainly has the most demoralizing effect upon those who may be addicted to it; and, once victimized, it seems that the greater the determination with which one tries to avoid it, the more will one foster the habit. Because the fear of shanking, by contracting the swing, induces shanking, the evil is cumulative, living upon itself. It is for this reason that I advise golfers who have never shanked to read no farther here. Shanking is a thing to cure, but not something to think about preventing.

Because it is a part of the justification for my existence that I do such things, although I have never shanked a shot in my life, I have given a good deal of thought to the possible causes and cures. So I was especially pleased to learn that a simple suggestion of mine, relayed to one of the finest woman golfers in the South, and intelligently applied by her, enabled her to stop her shanking, and to regain her confidence almost immediately. Unfortunately, everyone will not be able to effect a cure so readily, but that is not the fault of the remedy.

Shanking usually appears first in the shorter shots, where the common tendency is toward wooden wrists; but wherever it appears, the cause is the same, either failing to cock the wrists during the backswing, or failing to retain the cock long enough coming down. The players most likely to shank are those who employ short backswings in which there is a minimum of hand and wrist movement. When swinging the club in this way, upon arriving at the point where the blow must be delivered, the player feels the lack of this means of adding speed to the club head. He tries to make up for it by an effort in the shoulders and arms, and immediately shoves the socket of the club toward the ball. The cure, of course, is to assure a full cocking of the wrists during the backswing and to retain the greater part of this angle during the first half of the downswing.

It would be difficult to find a golfer more despairing than one who has run into a fit of shanking. A shanked iron shot is, of course, utterly ruinous; and the fear of producing such a result with every swing brings about a tension in the very muscles that ought to be relaxed and active. Becoming afraid to trust himself to swing the club freely, the poor victim squeezes it hard with his hands, and so makes more likely the occurrence of the dire result he is trying to avoid.

I have seen a player good enough to win a state championship once, and reach the final on another occasion, shank ten iron shots in one round of that final. I once saw, unbelievable though it may be, a competitor in an Open championship shank two putts in a round of the tournament. I am told that J. H. Taylor, the great English professional, once gave up golf for over a year because he could not stop shanking. All of which goes to show that a great part of the evil is in the mind. It is a most difficult thing to stop once it has taken a good hold. But the player who uses his hands and wrists properly and actively need have little worry.

CHAPTER TEN

1   RECOVERY SHOTS   157

2   THE MENTAL SIDE OF BUNKERS   158

3   TECHNIQUES OUT OF SAND   159

4   OUT OF THE ROUGH   162

5   DOWNHILL AND UPHILL LIES   164

6   AGAINST THE WIND   166

7   PUSH SHOTS   168

8   RELIEVING TENSION   169

9   FOR LEFT-HANDERS   171

10 THE INFLUENCE OF GOLF COURSE DESIGN   173

Bunker Play

CHAPTER TEN

I   RECOVERY SHOTS

The average golfer has always to fight tension; never may he feel entirely comfortable, or enjoy a complete confidence in his ability to make the shot required. This feeling of uncertainty makes him tighten up; and even after he has schooled himself to obtain a measure of relaxation in playing the accustomed strokes, he finds it hard not to become unduly alarmed when an unusual or difficult situation confronts him.

This applies with particular force to recovery work—from bunkers and long grass—and it is responsible in great part for the unwarrantable losses suffered from one bad shot. I think it is safe to say that the man who scores between 95 and 100 usually loses about ten strokes per round because of his failure to recover as well as he ought to, even in proportion to his limited ability. Tension, uncertainty, and fear take from him a heavier toll than they have any right to exact.

The tightening-up process as the player enters a bunker or long grass shortens his backswing considerably; usually, too, he feels the need of exerting some extra force in order to get the ball out. Thus he produces a short, hurried, ill-timed stroke that fails because of its inaccuracy. Brilliant recoveries to the edge of the hole are not for this man, but, under the conditions met in nine cases out of ten, there is no reason why a moderately successful recovery should not be within the reach of anyone. Most failures from bunkers, or rough, result from topping, and this is so because tension has upset the stroke.

I have said before that too much ambition is a bad thing to have in a bunker; the same holds true when playing from long grass. It is always difficult to resist the temptation to attempt to make up immediately for any mistake. When there is a long shot to be made, the average person will invariably try his luck with a club that he knows is unsafe. The one idea in playing from rough is to be certain of getting the ball up quickly enough to escape the grass. If this will not reach the green, it will be better to be a few yards short than to be still in the rough.

That a ball played from long grass will roll an abnormal distance, unless the turf be sodden, is a fact not often enough accounted for. Playing on fast ground, I have seen distances made with a five-iron or four-iron out of rough that would have required a two-iron or one-iron if played in a normal way from the fairway—and the shot could be played with assurance that it would clear the grass.

2   THE MENTAL SIDE OF BUNKERS

To be out of practice is good for one's golf game in no particular, but the greatest difference is always noted in the play around the greens. Often, after a long layoff, a considerable improvement may be wrought in the playing of the long shots, requiring complete relaxation and very little delicacy; but as the play comes closer to the hole, and the need for touch and delicate control become more exacting, the one who has not been in intimate contact with his clubs for a great while will surely suffer. There is a great difference between the accuracy required to place a full iron shot on a fair-sized green and that needed to guide a ten-foot putt into the cup.

At Winged Foot in 1929, what troubled me most was the bunker play around the greens. On every course, the weight and fineness of the sand is likely to be different, and, since almost every shot from sand is played according to the character of the surface upon which the ball rests, the niceties of bunker play vary for almost every course. In other words, although the fundamentals of the stroke remain the same, the success of the shot depends entirely upon the exactness with which the resistance of the sand is estimated.

Almost everyone had trouble that year with Winged Foot's bunkers. I saw very few who were at all certain of themselves in the light, fluffy sand. One of these was Harry Cooper, and Harry did what no one else troubled to do—he spent ten minutes each day before his round playing shots from the big bunker in front of the eighteenth green of the club's other course; when he went out to play, his practice made it easy for him to figure exactly how much sand to take behind the ball, in order to reach the desired distance. The rest of us would have done well to follow Harry's example.

It is almost impossible to exaggerate the disturbing effect upon one's entire game that can be produced by uncertainty concerning one's ability to recover well from bunkers around the green. The great value of a hazard is not that it catches a shot that has been missed, but that it forces a miss upon the timid player; its psychological worth is greater than its penal value. How much greater is this mental effect when the player knows that he has not the ability to recover if he makes a mistake. Every player knows this feeling; he also knows how comforting it is to feel that he can always blast from a trap to within reasonable putting distance of the hole. In the latter state of mind, he may hit his second shots firmly, with no gripping fear of what may happen; he feels that he may take a risk with an even chance of getting his four, even if the second shot should find a bunker.

3   TECHNIQUES OUT OF SAND

I have always considered that Freddie McLeod, who won the National Open Championship in 1908, was one of the most spectacular bunker players who ever lived; but Freddie and I have for years carried on a good-natured argument concerning the soundness of the shot he habitually employs. I have been willing to admit that Freddie can do wonders with it, but he has not agreed that in the hands of the average golfer it might prove a source of danger to the lives of his companions as well as to his score.

Playing from a clean lie in sand near the green, Freddie lays his niblick well off and takes a good, healthy swing. His club takes a mere feather of sand under the ball, so that the shot comes up with a terrific amount of spin; usually the ball drops past the hole and comes back toward it, often stopping very close indeed.

But when the average player finds his ball in a bunker, his chief aim should be to get it out in one stroke. He cannot expect to fulfill the exacting requirements of the shot as Freddie McLeod plays it. Instead of taking a feather of sand beneath the ball, he wants to be certain, first, of getting his club sufficiently under the ball to get it up, and second, of hitting hard enough to get it out of the bunker.

Laying the face of the club well off provides valuable insurance. In this way, it is possible to hit harder with the knowledge that taking too little sand will be less likely to send the ball over the green; but because the full blast produces a steep pitch, it is nevertheless a lob without spin, and it will roll. The heavy cushion of sand between the ball and the face of the club removes any possibility of backspin.

A great many players, adept in recovering from bunkers, employ what I call a modified or controlled blast. The backswing is on the long side, but the club is merely floated into the sand behind the ball; the cushion of sand is relatively light, and the shot comes up with some backspin. It is not so risky as McLeod's shot, but nevertheless requires a nice judgment of sand and club head speed to be brought off with consistent success. That this and other shots can be useful does not alter the fact that the full blast is the safest way of getting a ball out of a bunker.

Fred McLeod used to play another shot I admired. One day when we were playing a practice round at St. Anne's, he found his ball lying in a heel mark in a bunker some fifty or sixty yards from the green. Anyone else, I think, would have tried to hit sharply down upon the back of the ball with a lofted club.

But Freddie played an outright blast with a five-iron. The wall of the bunker was not high; his ball came out with plenty of run and finished neatly on the green.

To be really expert in recovering from any kind of trouble, including bunkers, a player must possess a certain amount of ingenuity in addition to a highly developed sense of club control. Many of the shots made from such places are not golf shots at all, but are acts of club manipulation possibly never tried before. The player who can handle his tools and has a spark of inspiration can often do wonders.

Long ago Tommy Armour asked me which I considered to have been the greatest shot I ever played. "When it meant something," he added. It did not take me long to nominate the iron shot from the bunker on the seventeenth hole at St. Anne's that enabled me to nose out Al Watrous in the British Open of 1926. The shot was about 175 yards across a number of other bunkers and dunes. I had a clean lie in the sand, and the shot was hardly more difficult than any blind second of the same length; but I did get a thrill out of it because it would have made such a lot of difference if the blade of my iron had taken the smallest speck of sand before it struck the ball.

"I rather expected you to name that one," said Tommy. "You know, I asked Hagen the same question, and he also named a bunker shot, out of the cross bunker on the fifteenth at Sandwich." I remember the bunker perfectly, having been in it a number of times, and the shot almost as well, although I did not see it.

When Hagen put his second in that bunker in the last round, he needed a five there, and three pars to finish, to beat the lowest total already in, and, apparently, to win the championship. He found his ball lying cleanly in the middle of the bunker, with the pin perhaps thirty yards away, about in the middle of the green. But the bunker is a formidable one; it is not so very large nor so awfully deep, but the front bank overhangs so that a ball close underneath it is scarcely playable.

The option for Hagen here was to play a safe blast, get his five, and still have to play the last three holes in par, or to take a desperate chance in the hope of getting a four, thus providing a marginal stroke that might well be needed on the finishing holes. He studied the shot with the utmost care, changed clubs at least twice, and ended by playing the most perfect chip imaginable; the ball stopped a foot from the hole, and he finished in par to win.

It was a big gamble, which for a less capable and confident player would have been suicidal; had his club even nicked the sand behind the ball, it was probable that the next shot would have been played from underneath the overhanging ledge, in which case a six would have been difficult to get. Hagen thought of this, but he felt that he could bring off the shot, and that the stroke, if gained, would be worth the risk. The knowledge that he probably had a stroke in hand would certainly make the last three pars a lot easier. As it turned out, he actually needed the four, for George Duncan, finishing late with a splendid round, had only to have a four, which he just failed to get, on the last hole to tie.

The short shots off clean sand, like Hagen's, are the most treacherous in golf. The long ones, like mine, are not so bad, for then the main thing is to strike a descending blow, as you would from the fairway—and if you take it heavy, you are hitting hard enough to get out of the bunker anyway. But the delicate stroke, if it fails, fails completely, and what is more, usually puts the ball against the face of the bunker, in a really difficult spot. So the failure may cost two or three strokes instead of one.

The average golfer should hope that he may never get a clean lie in a bunker around the green, for surely the temptation will prove too great for him. Let him always find his ball just a little bit down into the sand so that necessity, rather than his own strength of character, may cause him to take a lofted club and blast his way out.

4   OUT OF THE ROUGH

The average golfer, when he finds himself with a close lie, or with his ball lying deep in heavy grass, and a shot of 150 yards or so to a closely guarded green, is at a loss concerning the shot to play. The first thing that crosses his mind is that he must lose some length because of the lie of the ball, since it is not sitting high where he can hit it squarely. With this thought, and with the idea of compensating for this loss, he will select for the shot a stronger club than he would use if the ball were lying well.

Ordinarily, it is dangerous for a player of whatever ability to force an iron to its ultimate limit, but the situation I have described is one where such a thing is necessary. There are a number of reasons for this, all of which should be understood by the player who hopes to work out from troubles where the shots he learns on the practice tee have to be varied a little, or supplemented with a bit of ingenuity.

When the ball is lying in heavy grass, or in a small hole or depression, it becomes necessary to swing the club in a sharply descending arc—literally to dig the ball out of the haven it has found. This necessity takes loft off the club—hooding or closing the face until a five-iron becomes effectively a four-iron, and a four as strong as a three from a normal lie.

Now when it comes to hitting the ball, let us see what happens. The ball is lying so that it is apparent to the player that force will be required to dig it out, and, whether intentionally or not, he is going to hit it a good bit harder than he would ordinarily. There is no possibility, theoretical or practical, that any sort of half or spared shot can be played to offset the decrease in the loft of the club which I have mentioned.

This much takes care of the range of the shot, but there is one other argument in favor of using the more lofted club.

Everyone knows how impossible it is to play a backspin shot from a heavy lie, the grass cushion between the club and the ball preventing the clean contact needed to impart spin. So in order to stop the shot within reasonable or calculable limits the player must depend entirely upon elevation, and no club straighter than a four-iron will do the trick. If he can't make the distance with the four-iron, in nine cases out of ten he would do best to play safe, rather than attempt the use of a more powerful club.

It is often surprising what distances can be reached from long grass with a lofted club. I remember one shot in particular I played at Winged Foot that surprised me as much as anyone else. On the twelfth hole of the playoff, I pulled my drive to the rough behind a hill and beyond sight of the green. The hole is guarded at the left by a huge bunker which extends about half-way across the putting surface. The hole is about 470 yards in length, and my drive could not have traveled over 230 yards. I thought I had no earthly chance of reaching the green.

With the intention of whacking the ball out, over the hill, into position in front of the opening to the green, I selected a four-iron and hit the shot over the top of the hill to the left of the big tree standing on the edge of the fairway. But when I reached the green, I found my ball less than a foot off the putting surface. The shot with a four-iron had traveled at least 230 yards, aided by the tremendous roll produced by the heavy grass. Had I been in the fairway, I should have needed a spoon, at least, to make the same distance.

So instead of a stronger club, when playing from a cuppy or heavy lie, it is best to use a more lofted iron, making sufficient allowance so that the ball can be hit a smashing blow. For the exigencies of a situation of this kind, it is necessary to force the club to a degree which would never be good practice under ordinary circumstances.

5 DOWNHILL AND UPHILL LIES

The chief difficulty in downhill or uphill lies is in resisting the influence of the slope upon the transference of the weight of the body. To play either kind of stroke successfully, the player must either move against gravity, or hold himself back despite its pull. When playing a downhill, or hanging lie, the big problem is to stay back of the ball, and to resist the tendency induced by the sloping ground, to move the weight over to the left leg during the backswing; in the other situation, when the lie is uphill, the inclination is to fall back upon the right leg in the act of hitting, and so to strike in an upward direction. To play either kind of shot correctly, the player must learn to handle his body weight against the slope.

I do not think that altering the location of the ball by addressing it more off the right foot, or off the left, is likely to be helpful. The best rule is to take the stance and make the address so that the position is entirely comfortable. It was only occasionally, when playing a lofted club from such a lie, that I made the least conscious alteration in the positions of my feet with respect to the ball, and even then the concession was to comfort.

When playing downhill, it is important to remember that the ball cannot be picked up cleanly and lofted into the air; there is no way to get the club under it so that it can be struck upward. If it is to be got up with a wood club of little loft, it must be smashed down, so that the speed and the spin will cause it to rise. Obviously, this is one of the most exacting shots in the game, and the player who lacks the ability to hit hard and accurately will do well to go to a more lofted club; but even then the mechanics of the stroke are still the same.

The weight of the body must be held back during the backswing, and in starting down, the cock of the wrists must be retained. The blow must be descending, and its success will depend upon how well the player times his movement down the slope. In an extreme case, striking downward with the slope gives the body such an impetus that the player must take a step or two in the direction of the stroke in order to maintain his balance. The timing of this performance is not always easy, but there is no better way.

An uphill lie looks easy, and most players like it, but it does bring about an astonishing number of topped shots. Only the knowledge that it is necessary, supported by the determination to do so, will ever cause the player to move off his right foot up the slope as he swings into the ball. In almost every case, he will stay back on his right leg, and strike upward or across the ball from outside to in.

It may help a great deal to recognize the tendencies produced by situations of this nature, in order to be better able to guard against them. There ought to be in the player's mind a clear picture of how he wants his club face to be moving as it strikes the ball. Hitting downward from a hanging lie produces in almost every player a tendency to slice, because of cutting across the ball with the face of the club open. Playing uphill, the tendency will be to pull, because the face of the club is more likely to be closed. In either case, it will be very helpful to make an effort to swing through precisely on a line toward the hole.

6   AGAINST THE WIND

There is probably no shot in the game that bothers the average golfer so much as any shot into a head wind, where distance is of importance. Of all the hazards likely to be encountered on a golf course, wind is the most formidable for nine-tenths of those who play the game, because of its disturbing effect upon the mind. It is simply impossible, and understandably so, for an inexperienced player to maintain his mental equilibrium in the face of a strong wind.

Two things are most natural to do in this situation; one, to press the shot in order to make up the distance the wind takes away; the other, to try to hit the ball low so that it will escape the effect of the wind. The first of these, pressing, is, of course, fatal; the second is all right for the expert, but usually bad for the ordinary player, because he does not know how to accomplish his aim.

Now let's just stop and look at the thing for a moment. There is no way for me or anyone else to tell a man how he can hit a golf ball as far against the wind as he can with it, or in calm air; it simply cannot be done; so let's not consider this as a possibility. If we suppose that a certain player, at his ultimate, can reach a four-hundred-yard hole in two shots when there is no wind, then if the wind against takes ten yards off each shot, his limit will be reduced to 380 yards, and the four-hundred-yard hole will be beyond his reach. Most likely, if the hole actually measured twenty yards more than his limit, in calm air, he would not worry about reaching it; then let him regard the wind as adding just so many yards to the hole.

I prefer to regard the wind hazard in just this way—to treat it as part of the golf course—and to direct my efforts toward doing the best I can with respect to it. The main thing I think about is holding the ball on line. I try to get as much distance as I possibly can, with safety, but I never try to do more than I can. Direction is always of the first importance, and since an opposing wind magnifies errors in striking, it allows fewer liberties than could be taken at other times.

I think the best advice, when hitting a shot into a breeze, is to take things even a bit more quietly than usually, the very opposite of pressing. Primarily, of course, the reason for this is to give better direction, but it will also be found, surprisingly perhaps, that in this way the actual loss of distance will be lessened.

It is a most natural thought that a very low drive flies best into a breeze. In fact, there is one thing far more important than elevation—the trajectory of the flight of the ball. Those who yield to the inclination to hit the ball sharply down into a wind, soon discover that this kind of stroke does not actually keep the shot low; it merely starts the ball out close to the ground, but when it travels a distance, it begins to rise on the wind, and when it drops, it comes straight down; it has no ability whatever to bore its way along; it is at the mercy of even a light breeze.

Sometime when the opportunity comes, stand directly behind one of the best pros when he is hitting a drive against the wind and watch the flight of the ball. You will see the ball come up, and it may even go comparatively high—but you will notice that it has no abrupt rise just before it drops. The ball will almost seem to be looping over in the air, and when it strikes the ground it will be still going forward.

This sort of flight is not accomplished by hitting the ball down. The best stroke is one that takes the ball almost squarely in the back, while the club head is moving just about parallel to the ground; it applies only a very little backspin to the ball; and the more it can be made a sweep, instead of a sharp hit, the better.

7   PUSH SHOTS

It has not been difficult to cause a majority of golfers to understand that the controlled shot in golf—the shot intended to
carry some amount of backspin—is accomplished by a stroke that
brings the club head against the ball on the descending arc. Almost
everyone recognizes the divot-taking stroke the expert employs
with his iron clubs; so it is common knowledge that with these
implements it is proper to hit down. But in this respect, as in
many others, the degree to which the thing is done is of great
importance; it is impossible to think of a golfing virtue that cannot
be exaggerated or emphasized into a fault.

When I was a small boy, twelve or thirteen years old, I remember being much inspired by an article over Harry Vardon's
signature describing the correct method of executing a "push shot."
Prior to that time, I had heard a lot about the push shot and
had read numerous mentions of it, but I had never seen one played
—that is, as I had conceived it—although I had watched some
pretty fair players, among them old Harry himself. I even had
asked Stewart Maiden about it, but Stewart was never fond of
frills and had always put me off with some joking response.

So when I ran across this article of Vardon's, I decided to
give the push shot a try. I read the piece through, then reread
it; then I boarded an electric car and took the article with me
to a practice tee at East Lake. Stewart was giving a lesson on an
adjoining tee, but I dared not interrupt him; soon I became so
occupied with my article and the push shot that I forgot anyone
was near. The idea, it seemed, was to deliver a sharply descending
blow that would produce a low-flying shot that would bring up
quickly after striking the ground. The low trajectory was all I
was ever able to get. I was moving yards of turf at each stroke,
and giving my wrists an awful pounding, but I continued to hook,
smother, and top shots indiscriminately.

I was still taking myself seriously when I heard a soft chuckle behind. I turned at the sound and found Stewart perched on a bench, with cap cocked up on the back of his head and having the time of his life watching me. As I looked back, he chuckled again. "What are ye trying to do, Robin? Move the golf course?" was all he ever said, but I have never since troubled about the push shot.

I confess that to this day, I do not know if the push shot ever existed as a shot distinct from the ordinary low-flying iron shot we employ today to meet certain conditions. I am certain of one thing, which is that Harry Vardon never intended that the shot should be played as I attempted to play it. I am familiar with the low iron shot, played somewhat less than full, into a head wind; this shot is "hit down" slightly more than the perfectly straightforward type, but ever so slightly more.

I believe this was Vardon's meaning that I decided to go one better, like the patient who thought that if a tablespoonful of medicine would do him good, the whole bottle taken immediately would effect a cure. At any rate, for better, for worse, Stewart Maiden laughed me out of any further concern with the push shot. After that little experience, whenever anyone mentioned it to me I would change the subject as quickly as possible.

8 RELIEVING TENSION

Because tension is the golfer's worst enemy, and the problem of remaining completely relaxed in order to complete a rhythmic swing his most difficult task, I am going to try to set out a few simple rules that will be of help in loosening up, regardless of the mechanical precision of the swing. We all want to develop a swing free of imperfections, but even the most perfect swing must have rhythm, and the most imperfect one may be made fairly effective by the addition only of a sense of timing.

Here are the rules:

1. Grip the club lightly. Hold it mainly in the fingers, so that it can at all times be controlled and kept from turning in the hands without tautening the forearm muscles. But don't squeeze it. If you begin by gripping lightly, the hands will automatically tighten their hold as the progress of the swing makes this necessary. Make certain that you can feel the club head.

2. In addressing the ball, arrange the posture as naturally and as comfortably as possible. Avoid strain in the position as much as you can. Don't bend over too far, don't reach for the ball, don't stiffen the legs, and don't spread the feet. These seem to be a lot of "don'ts," but in reality they are merely saying, "Stand erect, let the arms hang naturally from the shoulders, and bring the ball close enough to be reached comfortably."

3. Use the legs and hips in beginning the backswing. Don't begin by picking the club up with the hands and arms. Swing the club back and give the hips a full windup. If an ample use of the important muscles in the waist and back is not made, the effort will be too great and the swing will lose its smoothness.

4. Be sure that the backswing is long enough. This gives the downswing plenty of time to get up speed before impact. A backswing that is too short inevitably leads to hurry and tension.

5. Start the downswing in leisurely fashion. Don't hit from the top of the swing. If the backswing has been of ample length there is no need to be in too much hurry coming down. Let the acceleration be smooth and gradual.

6. When it comes time to hit, don't leap at the ball. Let the club head do some of the work. Think of giving it speed and then let it float against and through the ball. Remember Newton's law that a body in motion tends to continue its motion in a straight line until acted upon by outside forces. Be careful of what "outside forces" you set up in trying at the last moment for that extra distance. Keep on swinging until the ball has had a good start down the fairway.

I have seen any number of players with terrible swings who obtained good results from a sense of rhythm and timing and nothing more; it is truly amazing how far one can go if he can only keep from tightening up. The effort to hit hard, instead of increasing the power of the swing, usually finishes in a sort of shove as what should have been the propelling force is expended too soon. The more leisurely swing, conserving this energy and discharging it where it will do the most good, yields more yards with considerably less effort.

9 FOR LEFT-HANDERS

Frankly, I cannot assign any very convincing reasons why a person should not play just as well left-handed as right-handed. Any number of objections to the left-handed method have been urged, but it seems to me that few of them, if any, have any real meat in them. One golfing physician advanced the theory that the swing of a left-handed player compressed the region around his heart and, therefore, impaired his physical efficiency. This one I should not attempt to pass judgment on, for I know nothing of the possible effect of whatever compression might result. But I do feel that some of the other reasons are patently unsound. In this class I would place the idea that golf courses are laid out for right-handed golfers and are, therefore, more severe upon the unfortunate who may prefer to stand on the other side of the ball. The only two considerations that might work to the advantage of the right-hander are that he can obtain superior clubs, and possibly more intelligent instruction because most of the good pros themselves happen to play in this way. Apart from these, it would appear that the only concern would be the comfort or preference of the individual.

The general prejudice that has grown up against the left-handed method has been fostered by the knowledge that there are in the world very few really expert players who play the game left-handed. It seems to me that we need look for no occult reason for this. Considerably fewer than one person of each ten thousand who play golf deserves an expert rating. I do not know the exact figures, but I should say that there would not be more than one left-handed player in each three hundred. If we take it at one in three hundred and the number of golfers in the United States at seven and a half million, we should expect to have, according to my figures, seven hundred and fifty experts, which is high, three of whom might be left-handed.

One thing that some people assume, I do not know to be the case; namely, that the left arm of a right-handed person is necessarily weaker than the right. That, it seems to me, would not follow just because he might have a greater use of the right in certain performances requiring a more perfect control. It is my idea that the left arm should control the golf swing, but its function can be performed without the player's having the use of it that would be required for accurate throwing, writing, or any number of other acts accomplished normally by the right. I conceive that there are certain definite reasons why the left arm should take the club back and why it should dominate the hitting stroke, and I do not admit that a right-handed person would be able to pull the club down from the top, in backhanded fashion, with any more powerful effect with his right than with his left arm, even though he might be able to throw better with the right.

And here is another thought. Remember that the motion of the left arm is simple—straight back and straight down—and that the use of the right has to be a good bit more delicate. Would not a right-handed person be better able to perform those more delicate actions with his right hand than with his left, as he would be required to do if he were to switch over? I wrote in an earlier chapter that I thought that a golf swing was somewhat like the gait of a trotting horse in that it was not able to be directed by natural impulses; and the hand and arm that is not working on a track and has to be watched is the right. I think that I, who am very right-handed, would prefer that it be so.

No, I do not believe that a person who is naturally right-handed would be happy playing golf left-handed, even though he might have been successful batting left-handed; there is a great difference between the batting swing and the golf stroke. But I do believe that our prejudice against the left-handed style of play is groundless. If I were just beginning the game and should find myself definitely more comfortable on one side of the ball than the other, I should remain on that side.

10 THE INFLUENCE OF GOLF COURSE DESIGN

In modern golf course design here in America, we have come to insist upon complete visibility from the second shot, fairways and greens well defined by bunkers or other hazards, and well-watered putting surfaces that will hold almost any kind of pitching shot; and then we spend a great deal of money in smoothing out undulating fairways, and in providing a perfect turf to assure good lies. The tendency has been to remove, as far as possible, all uncertainty from the game, to bring it closer to an exact science.

The first effect of this has been to emphasize the importance of form. When every wayward shot suffers an immediate penalty, one realizes at once that what one needs most is a sound, reliable method that can be reproduced time and again without serious error.

The next impression, because all greens hold well, is that a variety of strokes is not needed; because a pitch will nearly always do, our young golfer has only one shot to learn, and so becomes more proficient in its use. From tee to green, what is wanted, and all that is wanted, is mechanical precision. When a well-played shot always, or nearly always, gets its reward, it is not difficult to induce a young man to concentrate upon form and accurate striking.

This much, of course, is excellent, because it suggests a beginning where the beginning should be made; but there should be a realization that there is something beyond. Courses of this kind, playable in only one way, day after day, do not teach a player to think or to use his imagination, to invent ways of working himself out of difficulties. Having learned to pitch, for example, when he finds that his pitches won't stop, he doesn't know what to do. Until he gets experience, he will not think to examine a slope to find a way to run his ball up close to the hole.

I do believe, though, that on the whole, our American-type

course provides excellent training in shotmaking; the rest can come later. I do not believe that we should set such value as we do upon good form if we habitually played on courses where the uncertainties of the game were greater.

SECTION TWO

PLAYING THE GAME

CHAPTER ELEVEN

1 GOLF AS RECREATION 179

2 HOW TO PRACTICE 181

3 GETTING THAT CERTAIN FEEL 183

4 THE VALUE OF SIMPLICITY 185

5 RESOURCEFULNESS AND JUDGMENT 187

6 SLOW PLAY 189

7 PRACTICE SWINGS 190

8 SCORING 191

9 THE IMPORTANCE OF PUTTING 193

Warming Up

CHAPTER ELEVEN

I GOLF AS RECREATION

The golfer with a fairly good swing who never seems able to score well is a familiar figure on any course. In many respects, he is in the same boat with the tournament player who burns up the course in practice rounds, but does nothing in the actual competition. Obviously, there is a great deal more to playing golf than merely swinging the club.

There is scarcely one golfer of the so-called average class who could not benefit from an effort to school himself in applying good sense, judgment, and a little intelligent thinking to his game; and this without reference to the mechanics of the swing. Merely by adopting measures that will help get a consistently high rate of performance from what ability he has, a surprising improvement can be made.

The trouble with all of us, who grumble over the game and thus spoil an otherwise pleasant afternoon with congenial friends, is that we do not understand the game, nor ourselves. In this, we could take a number of lessons from the dub. For no matter how good we may be, if we should fancy that we have mastered golf to the extent that we can go out day after day and play as we please, then we are greater fools than ought to be left at large.

A skillful golfer, who knows what he is about, can often play himself back to his game in the course of a round; but the average player, when he goes out for an afternoon, would best leave all his tinkering and theorizing behind. Too many come out eager to try some new discovery made while shaving, or lying awake in bed, and, instead of going to the practice tee to find out if the idea has any merit, they set out hopefully to beat their record for the course. It would be difficult to think of a more infallible way of spoiling what might have been an enjoyable game.

The virtues of golf as a pastime and a means of recreation have been appropriately extolled. But no one, with more than the barest outside chance of being believed, is going to tell me, or any other golfer, that he gets any fun out of hacking around a golf course in ten or more strokes above his normal score. The ninety player does not expect to break eighty; he ought to be, and usually is, satisfied to play a game that is reasonably good for him. But when he plays a really bad round, and drags himself into the locker room, it is easy to see that he is tired and disgusted, and has done anything but enjoy himself.

It seems to me that there are two reasonable ways in which a man may take his golf. If he has the time and inclination to do so, he may set out to give the game a proper amount of serious study and effort, with a view toward elevating himself beyond the average-golfer class; or, if he has only a very limited amount of free time, as many have, he may be content to knock around with his regular companions who play about as he does, in search of a little fun. But it will not do to mix the two, especially to hang the ambitions of the first man upon the labors of the latter.

When we come to the all-important matter of getting real enjoyment out of the playing of the game, I think we will find that all must employ the same set of rules. To find enjoyment, we must produce a round fairly close to our usual standard. To do this with a fair degree of consistency, no matter to which class we belong, we must avoid experiment, refuse to try anything new, and play the game instead of practicing it.

The best single piece of advice I could give any man starting out for a round of golf would be "take your time," not in studying the ground, and lining up the shot, but in swinging the club. Strive for smoothness, strive for rhythm; but unless you are something of an expert, save "monkeying" with your hip turn, your wrist action, and the like, until you can get on a practice tee where you can miss a shot without having to play the next one out of a bunker.

2 HOW TO PRACTICE

Never should I knowingly discourage any man from trying to learn to swing a golf club correctly, for I think the game is well worth whatever effort one may make toward this end. But if one is not willing to take lessons and practice, he will do better to make up his mind to worry along with what he has, rather than to mess up all his rounds with misguided tinkering.

To stand upon a tee for hours banging away mechanically and monotonously at ball after ball is certainly trying on the nerves; it also is a waste of time. It is exercise, to be sure, but it is exercise only in the sense that digging ditches and plowing fields is exercise. There can be no enjoyment in it, and from such labors, one usually goes home with a tired soul and blistered hands.

Practice must be interesting, even absorbing, if it is to be of any use. Monotony palls, and nothing can be more monotonous than playing over and over the same shot from the same place. I used never to practice, simply because I could never find a way to hold my attention upon what I was doing. The first dozen or so shots I would hit painstakingly and thoughtfully, and then the rest would be sent off one after the other at such a pace that soon I would be out of breath, perspiring, and wholly disgusted.

The secret of beneficial practice is keeping a definite idea upon which to work. If you cannot think of some kink to iron out or some fault to correct, don't go out. And if there is a kink or a fault, as soon as it has been found and cured, stop immediately and don't take the risk of unearthing a new one or of exaggerating the cure until it becomes a blemish in itself. A man cannot do worse than to practice simply because he has nothing else to do.

Driving practice is, to me, the very hardest, because in approximating actual play, there is no direct target at which to aim. Playing from a level tee down an ordinary fairway is the least interesting phase of golf, and practice in this department is necessarily fatiguing. I very seldom gave a great deal of time to this sort of practice. If I found a difficulty which did not yield quickly, I usually tried to relieve the burden by mixing my shots. In other words, if I drove a dozen balls or so without discovering the trouble, I would cast the driver aside and hit a few balls with a spoon or an iron before going back to the recalcitrant member. In this way, I could usually start where I left off with a zest otherwise impossible.

I deem it worse than useless to practice with the irons from an ordinary tee or on an ordinary practice field. The iron clubs are properly for playing shots to the green, and therefore practice with them should be had with a green and a flag as the objective. There are difficulties in the way here because, on our crowded courses, a lone man playing balls to any regular green can be nothing but a nuisance to other players; also, he may be a decided pest to the greenskeeper if he practices from the fairway. But usually a time can be picked when play on the course is not heavy, and spots can be found off the fairway where the turf is sufficiently good. One might even persuade the directing authority to provide a few target areas on the practice field.

In practicing with the irons, it is always better to move about so that the distance and angle of the shot may vary. If you remain in the same spot, even granting that the stroke and scenery don't grow irksome, the playing of the accustomed shot will finally grow so mechanical that you may be misled into believing you have progressed beyond your actual attainment.

The above suggestions apply mainly when there is a particular shot that needs improvement or a particular fault that needs correcting. But there are other situations that demand a kind of practice, especially when, through lack of play, a man's game needs a little general polishing. The best way to put on these finishing touches is a nine-hole jaunt with your entire set of clubs, four or five balls, and a caddie. When you play a sour shot, you can play another ball, and you can drop and play others from any point you desire. In this way, you can obtain a greater variety of shots than you could be called upon to play in a half-dozen ordinary rounds.

Macdonald Smith is credited with saying that he always practiced the shot he was playing best; in other words, his practicing was done to cultivate good habits, rather than to correct bad ones. His idea may have been good for Mac, but I am sure his method would not suit the average man. Golf is such a curious game and form is so fleeting that there can be no better maxim than to leave alone what is doing well enough. There can be nothing more dangerous than tampering with a club that is working well, for, sooner or later, too much attention will spoil the machinery. The club is most likely performing satisfactorily because it inspires confidence in its owner, and the more it is used, the more likely it may be to betray that confidence.

Above all things, make your practice take an interesting form. Go out with a definite purpose and stay with your work only so long as that purpose remains definite. If you find it relaxing, or if the purpose is achieved, go home, and give your muscles and your head a rest. Nothing can be gained by tinkering with your swing after it has been once straightened out.

3   GETTING THAT CERTAIN FEEL

To determine just how hard to try to hit a golf ball in order to get the best results is often a perplexing problem. Everyone knows the dangers of pressing and the troubles one can encounter when trying to hit too hard. But the shoe can rub the other way, too, and the fellow who tries to swing too easily is often just as close to disaster. Somewhere between these two extremes is the happy middle ground the golfer must tread.

I cannot recall that I ever accomplished any really good scores or won any matches by trying to knock the cover off the ball. Good driving has been a part of all the really fine rounds I ever played. It is true that, except for those occasions when a putter goes phenomenally hot, a man must be driving well to score well. But all that is needed is ordinarily good length and a good deal of accuracy, the latter feature being by far the more important of the two.

I got as much fun as the next man from whaling a ball as hard as I could and catching it squarely on the button. But from sad experience I learned not to try this in a round that meant anything.

But there is the other extreme that is just as bad. Whenever one becomes too careful and begins to steer his shots, he can get into just as much trouble, and his trouble may be found a lot farther from the green than if he had taken a good, healthy swing. Easing up almost always leaves the left side in the way—there is not enough pull to get it around where it ought to be—and when the swing finds itself blocked, there is no way for it to go through cleanly and smoothly.

Of all the times that I have struggled around the golf course, there are a few easy rounds that stand out in my memory. These are the ones I should like to play over again, and it would not take long, for there are not that many. One at Sunningdale, England, one at East Lake in Atlanta, two at Augusta, Georgia (both in one day), one at Interlachen in Minneapolis, and that's about all. Other scores were as good, but no other rounds were as satisfying.

Strangely, perhaps, one thing stands out about all those rounds; I had precisely the same feel on each occasion; I was conscious of swinging the club easily and yet without interruption; my left side was moving through without hindrance, yet I was making no special effort to get it out of the way; in fact, I had to make no special effort to do anything.

Sunningdale came first. I did not recognize the symptoms, because I had never had them before. Then, the next year, we had an open tournament at East Lake. In warming up before the second round, I suddenly realized that I had the same feel I had had at Sunningdale—and it worked again. It is not unnatural that

I tried to get it every time I went out on the course, but only a few times did it come.

I think it is helpful to begin a round, or better still, to begin warming up for a round, swinging the club as easily as possible, gradually working up speed until you play yourself into a tempo that feels about right. After you have found the right rhythm for the driver, try to carry the same beat down through the other clubs. In other words, vary the selection of clubs for the fairway shots so they can be swung as nearly as possible in the same rhythm. If you are able to swing the driver easily and get a good solid contact and good direction, it is more than likely that on that particular day you will have better luck with your irons if you will take the stronger club and swing it easily also. If you find that in driving it is necessary to swing hard in order to move the left side out of the way, the chances are that the irons will be better if the more lofted clubs are chosen and swung more nearly with full force.

No matter how "average" one's game may be, there are always vast possibilities in this matter of finding the proper beat for a given day. It is really a sort of tuning-up process everyone can go through with profit. And always the start should be made on the low side, swinging easily at first, gradually increasing the speed until the thing begins to click. And remember, it is not length that is wanted so much as accuracy and consistency.

4 THE VALUE OF SIMPLICITY

It is quite natural for anyone writing or discoursing upon the ways and means of playing golf to devote some little attention to the way of an expert in controlling the shots. The temptation is almost irresistible to suggest how an intentional slice or hook can be brought off, and when writing of such things, the preceptor, for fear that the value of his advice will be too readily discounted, hesitates to admit that he ever, for himself, has any doubt concerning the success of such a shot. Some of us, I fear, give the impression that the difficulty of these strokes is only apparent, that they annoy us not a whit, and that we face them with quite as much assurance as the straightforward iron from the fairway.

John Duncan Dunn has remarked that one sees at an open championship precious few of these intricate shots so blithely described. Unquestionably, this is fact, and in it is much for the ordinary player to heed.

The straightforward shot is invariably the one to employ when anything of importance hangs on the result. When a great field starts out over the seventy-two-hole route, everyone knows that a few strokes foolishly wasted may lose a coveted prize. You may be sure that none takes any chances or employs any means of reaching the goal that has not been tried repeatedly and found reliable. Competition has no place for experimenters.

When there is a chance of bringing off an exceptional shot, the wise competitor always considers and appraises the penalty in case of failure. Thus, on a par five hole after a long drive, the green may be so situated, and other conditions such that a long, sliced brassie shot affords the only means of getting home in two. It will not require long for the experienced eye to see the possibility; but just the knowledge that he can intentionally slice a brassie shot is not enough to induce him to attempt the shot; the success of the shot will depend entirely upon the amount of the slice and the length of the shot. The first thing to be thought of is what will be the cost of failure. If a mistake will likely leave a simple pitch for a certain 5 and a possible 4, the shot will be tried; but if the trouble to be encountered is at all severe, the safer course will always be favored.

So, if the expert distrusts these shots, how unwise it is to describe the manner of execution to a less accomplished player without a few words of caution. Some time ago, I offered my explanation—I now offer the words of caution. It should be interesting to the average player to know what the better men are doing, but he will be better off to let his interest stop there. Golf simplified, and not full of complications beyond his ability, is what he should have.

Leo Diegel was the only man I ever knew who actually thrived on difficult shots. Diegel played nearly every shot with a slight fade or draw, scarcely ever using a straight flying shot; and, although I do not hesitate to say that Leo could do more with a golf ball than any other man, he was still one of the most erratic of golf's great players; his inconsistency was almost entirely attributable to his preference for the more intricate shots.

5   RESOURCEFULNESS AND JUDGMENT

Let a person post himself at any point on the course during the progress of an open championship, or of any really first-class tournament, and watch the entire field go by. Of these he will, of course, be impressed by the Palmers, Players, Nicklauses, and the others who bear illustrious names; but I am sure he will be surprised by the number of fine shots played by men of whom he has never heard; and if he is an intelligent observer, he will appreciate that these fine shots are not mere accidents. There will be unknown players in the parade whose swings bear every evidence of the excellence displayed by the most famous man in the field. What, then, is the difference between those who finish always near the top and those who sometimes finish not at all?

The answer, I think, is that the successful man carries a resourcefulness, and a quality of judgment, the lack of which dooms the other fellow, despite his mechanical skill, to a permanent place among the also-rans. Knowing what to do and when to do it is the necessary complement to mechanical skill that maintains a few men at the head of the procession, with many others clutching closely, but vainly, for their coattails.

Traveling about the country playing exhibition matches in various sections, the itinerant champion very often finds himself soundly drubbed, or sorely pressed, by the local pro of whom the mighty one had never heard until he set foot in the clubhouse. Yet, if the two men were set down upon a course with which neither was familiar, the unknown would have little chance. That is a factor which, if it were more generally appreciated, would considerably decrease the number of disappointments devoted friends experience upon the failure of their local pride to set the championship field back upon its heels. It is not easy to understand how 69's and 68's at home can be so easily converted into 80's on foreign soil.

This does not mean necessarily that the strange course requires a type of play of which the man is incapable; no, without doubt, in time, and in a not very long time, he could play the new course as well as his own. But he has not the faculty which the first-class player possesses of quickly sizing up the requirements of the shot and of choosing the club and the method of playing it. That is what I mean by resourcefulness and judgment. Skill alone may be enough to play a course so well known that such decisions are made automatically, but to conquer an unfamiliar layout, considerable work must be done by what lies between the ears.

Fortunately, sound judgment in golf can be acquired in much easier fashion than can mechanical skill; experience over various courses and under varied conditions will teach a lot to any man; if he can play the shots, the rest can be learned by proper thought and application.

The average golfer may ask what this has to do with him. Apparently little, but the point is that by training himself to visualize and plan each shot before he makes it, and by giving careful thought to his method of attack, he can improve his game more certainly than by spending hours on a practice tee. Some men, for one reason or another, can never learn to swing a golf club correctly; but everyone can improve in the matter of selecting the shot to be played.

The importance of good judgment is made no less because the average player has fewer shots at his command than the skillful professional. The problem is nevertheless the same—how best for the particular individual to play the particular shot. Good judgment must take into account the personal equation as well as the slope and condition of the ground and the location of bunkers and other hazards.

6 SLOW PLAY

There can be no odium attached to slow playing when the motives of grandstanding and of upsetting an opponent are eliminated—and these can be entirely eliminated from this discussion; but I regard it as a mistake, considering both the player's efficiency and the welfare of the game in general. Golf depends for its growth upon public interest, and competitions are designed to stimulate public interest. Nothing can be less entertaining to the spectator than a round of golf drawn out by minute examinations of every shot.

After all, the deliberation necessary depends entirely upon the man who is playing the game; it is his business to play the shot, and he should never be required to play until he is ready.

Some situations one finds on a golf course require some amount of study before the player can determine the best way to overcome the difficulty; but these are unusual. The vast majority of shots from the fairway are but repetitions of countless hundreds played before. At least, to one familiar with the course, as all tournament contestants are, the decision should be a matter of seconds.

There is one very cogent reason why the older heads and more prominent players should make an especial effort to avoid unnecessary delay; that is, because of the effect of their examples upon the youngsters coming along. Youth is naturally confident, and playing with assurance, is not so likely as the older man to quail at the difficulties of a shot.

Whenever I see a much-considered shot go astray, I can't help thinking of the lawyer who had unsuccessfully defended a client charged with murder. The trial had been long drawn out, lasting nearly a month, and the lawyer had made quite a lot of noise and stormed eloquently in his argument. Meeting a brother lawyer on the street a few days later, the case came up in discussion.

The lawyer, whose client had been convicted, asked his friend what he thought of his conduct of the trial. His friend replied, "Well, I think you could have reached the same result with a whole lot less effort."

More often than not, the first impression in golf is the best. There is no man capable of hitting a golf ball with sufficient exactness to warrant concern about the minute undulations a very close examination might reveal. If he can care for the difficulties he can see at a glance, he will have done well enough.

7 PRACTICE SWINGS

There is nothing in the rules of golf prohibiting a practice swing under any conditions or in any circumstances. Provided that nothing be done to cause the player to be guilty of improving his lie, touching the sand in a hazard, removing an obstruction or growing thing, or of doing some other act prohibited by the rules, he has the legal right to take as many practice swings as he chooses in whatever direction he may desire. Even in a bunker, he may swing the club as often as he likes, so long as he does not touch the sand or otherwise improve the lie of his ball. Many players are under the impression that a practice swing may not be taken within a club length of the ball, but the only requisite of this nature is that the absence of the intent to strike the ball must be clear.

While thus defining the player's legal rights, it is only fair to say that his moral right to make a nuisance of himself is not so clear. It is probably natural that a man playing golf is interested in nothing so much as his own game. It is also natural that he should attend to his opponent's game only enough to hope that said opponent will encounter enough trouble to cause him to lose the hole. But if he feels this way, he ought to remember that his companion probably entertains some such notions of his own play, and that he certainly has not come out to spend the greater part of the afternoon watching someone else take practice swings

and fiddle around over a golf ball in making preparations to strike
it. The ethics of the game allow each person a reasonable opportunity to play each shot carefully, but they demand also that
the player step up promptly to do his bit without unnecessary
delay.

The habitual practice swingers, and there are numbers of them,
have an uncanny talent for taking their swings at precisely the
wrong times. Everyone has had the experience and knows how
annoying it is hearing the swish of a club behind him just as
he is in the midst of his swing. He has to be very fond of the
culprit to restrain a desire to bash him on the head with the club,
even when he knows that the guilt is only of thoughtlessness.

8 SCORING

Why is it, someone asks, that so often after making an exceptionally good score on the first nine holes, a player
apparently loses all touch with his game and comes home in
astonishingly bad figures? Isn't it strange that this explosion should
occur when he is in his best stride? Apparently, there is a lower
limit fixed upon the score a given person may turn in, and if he goes
many strokes below his allotment in the early stages, it is more than
likely that the closing will even the count.

Yet it is no such law of averages, or anything like it, that is
responsible for the leveling process. It is almost impossible to
measure the force with which the awareness of a good score in
the making weighs down upon the performer. The nearer he
approaches his goal, the harder each shot becomes, until the
meanest obstacles appear almost insurmountable. There is far less
nervous strain involved in overcoming the effects of a bad start
than in maintaining the standard set by a well-made beginning.

This mental pressure is responsible more than anything else for
the fact that the third-round leader rarely finishes in front of an
Open Championship field. What presses him down is not that he
has "shot his bolt," as the saying is, for if the fourth round were

a separate affair with everyone starting even, he could probably do as well as anyone; but the thought of the few strokes' lead he must protect makes him overfearful and overcautious. The man drawing up from the rear, on the other hand, finds himself in an aggressive frame of mind, with nothing to think about except playing golf. Very often he can play himself into a winning position before he has time to appreciate the import of what he is doing.

The shopworn admonition to forget the last shot and play the one in hand was meant to apply as much to the good ones as to the bad. It is just as important to forget the 3's as the 6's.

I have never forgotten the comment made to me several years ago by a well-known professional. We had just heard at the clubhouse that Walter Hagen had run into a phenomenal string of sub-par holes. "You know, Bobby," said the pro, "the greatest thing about Hagen is that after he makes a few birdies he thinks he can keep on doing it, whereas if you or I do it, instead of continuing to play golf we begin to wonder if this isn't too good to be true. We begin to be suspicious of our good fortune and to expect a 6 or 7 to jump up any minute."

Of course, one may say that it is easy to understand why there should be a considerable mental strain in a tournament, but the same conditions do not bear upon a Saturday afternoon of golf. It is a different situation, of course, but every golfer knows what it means to beat his best score over his home course. The putt that turns the trick is fully as momentous, for the player, as the winning stroke in any championship.

In 1916, my best score at East Lake was 74, not in competition, of course, and like anyone else, every time I went out to play I tried to beat it. I tried all that summer and all the next year without success. I remember at least four occasions when I stood on the seventeenth tee needing only two pars, a 4 and a 3, not merely to beat 74, but to beat 70. Each time I arrived at that point, I began to think of what I was about to do, and each time I would use up just enough strokes to bring my total up to 74. It was two full years before I could break through the barrier raised by that 74. If I could have refrained from thinking about it, I should have probably beat it in a few months.

So the average player's difficulty in breaking 90 or 85 is no different from the expert's trouble when he tries to win a championship. When I hear a man censured for collapsing in the last round of a competition when he apparently had it won, I always want to ask the critic if he has ever had three 5's to beat his own best score and if he got them. Whether the score be 70 or 100 is of little moment. It's all a question of what it means.

9   THE IMPORTANCE OF PUTTING

The experiment of substituting eight-inch cups for the standard 4¼-inch size brings us back to the old contention that too much of the game of golf is played on the putting green. Someone is always trying to improve or reform something and golf has not escaped.

I remember some years ago a professional tournament played over an English course—Wentworth, I believe—in which an attempt was made to reckon points for accurate approach shots. A series of concentric circles was laid out around each hole and the players were awarded so many points for score, and in addition, a varying numer of points depending upon which circle they were able to hit with their second shots. Like the Florida experiment, this was a protest against the importance of putting in golf as it has always been played.

The argument runs something like this: Par is intended to represent perfect golf. The average par of an 18-hole course is, roughly, 72, and par figures always allow two putts to a green. Thus, in an 18-hole round, par figures allow the player 36 putts and 36 other shots distributed among his remaining clubs. Since one-half of the strokes of a perfect round of golf may be played with a putter, is there not too much premium placed upon skill with the club? Would not the distribution be fairer if the hole could be made of such size as to make one putt per green, instead of two, a reasonable allowance?

One answer to this is, of course, that excellence in driving and in iron play receives its reward as certainly as does excellence in putting. Often, of course, bad putting can nullify the advantage gained in other departments, but certainly a long, straight drive makes the second shot easier, and an accurate second shot places the player in winning position.

The advocates of the larger hole would eliminate from the game the unfair result coming about when one player holes a long putt and "steals" a hole from a man who has outplayed him to the green. Their contention is that the hole should be large enough so that the holing of any reasonable putt after a fine second shot would be practically certain. But they overlook the fact that the "thief" would then be holing from off the green and from bunkers quite as often.

The dub hails the larger cup with delight, because he conceives that he will no longer be blowing the short putts and that all the little ones that now rim the hole will begin to fall in. But here again the thing is entirely relative. Instead of rimming and missing from two, three, and four feet, he will experience the same disappointment when he misses from ten, twelve, and fifteen feet. No matter what we do to the hole, we will never cease to hear about the ball that might have gone in but didn't.

It seems to me that the larger hole might have just the opposite effect from that claimed for it, for I believe it would make more difference in the putting game for the man who was continually leaving himself away from the hole than for the fellow who is always banging his second shots up close. The second man seldom has to worry about taking three putts, even with the present hole size, and if he is at all a good putter, he will pick up a number of one-putt greens, whereas the other fellow, playing a bit wider on his approaches, will scarcely ever get down in one, except by accident and often, if his touch is not just right, he will be taking three.

I have no real fear that these experiments will lead to anything. I do not think that making the hole larger would make the game any better, but even if it would, I should still recall what I consider the best argument advanced against a change. I once heard someone say, when a discussion like this was going on, "Surely, go ahead and make the hole any size you please. But when you do, do not call the game golf."

CHAPTER TWELVE

1 TOURNAMENT PREPARATION 197

2 COMPETITIVE ATTITUDE 198

3 CONSISTENCY 202

4 EIGHTEEN-HOLE MATCHES 207

Competition

CHAPTER TWELVE

I   TOURNAMENT PREPARATION

There are two distinct kinds of golf—just plain golf and tournament golf. Golf—the plain variety—is the most delightful of games, an enjoyable, companionable pastime; tournament golf is thrilling, heartbreaking, terribly hard work—a lot of fun when you are young with nothing much on your mind, but fiercely punishing in the end.

Competition in any line of sport is today frightfully keen. In golf, both the professional and amateur fields embrace far more dangerous players than were to be found twenty years ago. The game is spreading like wildfire.

This means that to keep step with the field, from a competitive angle, is growing more and more difficult every year for the men who have businesses and professions to look after. One has either to enter a competition, conceding to his opponents the advantage of practice and preparation, or to take the time himself at the expense of other endeavors to play himself into form.

Aside from the time required for preparation, there is the equally important question of keenness. When a youngster embarks upon a career in competition, the whole thing is a great lark; no one knows who he is nor expects him to do anything; he can play to beat all if he likes, fight as hard as he can and congratulate himself if he makes a good showing. Being completely free of responsibility, he can have a great time. But let him begin to win and all this changes; he is now expected to do things; he carries a weight of responsibility on his shoulders; he is followed about the course, and if he fails, he is not allowed to forget it for a long time.

Of course, the first thing one must have in order to be successful in tournaments is a sound, reliable game. Yet this is a thing to be built up over a period of years, by patient study and practice on top of at least a moderate amount of natural aptitude. Like cramming for a final examination, a week or two of perspiring practice in preparation for a tournament is more likely to do harm than good; if the game is not already there, it is not likely to be acquired at the last moment.

On the other hand, to do too much experimenting on the eve of a tournament is always a bad thing. Many players beat themselves because they will not leave their swings alone long enough to play through the competition. Most of us have all the year to practice and experiment, to tinker with our swings and to improve our method. When a tournament comes along, it is time to forget all that, time to leave off experimenting, and, placing complete trust in the muscular habits we have acquired, to concentrate on "getting the figures."

The most important part of preparing for a tournament is to condition oneself mentally and physically so that it will be possible to get the most out of what game one possesses. Rigorous physical training is neither necessary nor beneficial. A physical condition that is too fine usually puts the nerves on edge. What one needs most is to play golf, to harden the golfing muscles, and to get the feel of the little shots around the green.

How much to play is something everyone must learn for himself. The happy state is one of complete familiarity with all the shots and clubs, and a keenness for the game that thrills in anticipation of the coming contest. Too little golf is bad, but too much is worse. To be jaded and stale before the tournament even begins is an entirely hopeless condition. Yet no one can say how much golf another can tolerate.

2   COMPETITIVE ATTITUDE

In every sport, and, I suppose, in almost every other line of endeavor, it is hard to separate and recognize the qualities that distinguish the great from the near-great—the men who succeed from those who just can't quite make it. In golf, this little difference, as telling as it may be, is yet so small that it is difficult to see that it can have a positive and consistent value.

I remember reading in an English newspaper after I had won the British Open at St. Andrews, an editorial that made a point of the slight margin of superiority shown by the winner of a tournament over the rest of the field. In this particular championship, I had won by the greatest margin I had ever had, yet as the editorial pointed out, my advantage of six strokes, however big it may have looked, when reduced to percentage, read only 2.105 per cent, or 1½ strokes in each round in which an average of a little less than seventy-two strokes were used.

I suppose it is consideration of a slender margin such as this that led J. H. Taylor to say that the difference between the winner and the near-winner is the ability on the part of the successful contestant to be ever on the lookout against himself. Never too certain of what the result may be, he plays not one shot carelessly or with overconfidence.

In competition, I have not regarded seriously the tendency of some people to endow golfers with superhuman powers. Because on occasions a few players have staged spectacular finishes to retrieve victory by last-minute rallies, I have heard it said of them that they are able to pull off whatever is necessary to win. Such an idea is absurd, for if these men were capable of playing golf as they willed, they would never place themselves so that they had to beat par to win; and when I hear someone criticized for cracking at the finish, I always think of the query Grantland Rice propounded at Scioto—whether it is better to blow up in the third round or the fourth. Every player has his bad patches in any seventy-two-hole journey. It is mainly a question of who averages up best over the entire route, and that, I think, is the feature the winner remembers and the field forgets.

When we begin to think in terms of the English editorial I have referred to, we must see the importance of each stroke, whether it be drive, approach, or putt; and we ought to see also that in a medal round to hole a long putt for a six is just as helpful as if it were for a three. It is every shot that counts.

In defining the difference between the great and the near-great, J. H. Taylor pointed out a lesson for every golfer. He was not merely explaining why some fine golfers win championships and others equally fine do not. He was telling you why you missed that easy pitch to the fourth green yesterday and why, after you had missed your second shot to the eighth, you took a seven instead of the five you should have had if you had played sensibly. All of us, from duffers to champions, would do better if we would play each stroke as a thing to itself.

It is difficult for a person who has not been mixed up in these things to understand what it means to play a competitive round against opponents who cannot be seen. In an Open Championship, one's imagination runs riot. A burst of applause or a cheer from a distant part of the course is always interpreted as a blow from some close pursuer, when it may mean no more than that some obscure competitor has holed a chip shot while another player's waiting gallery happened to be watching. It may not mean a thing, and even if it does, it can't be helped. But it is difficult to view it that way; one always feels that he is running from something without knowing exactly what nor where it is.

I used to feel that although I might make mistakes, others would not. I remember looking at the scoreboard before the last round of the 1920 Open, my first, and deciding that I must do a 69 at the most to have a chance. Actually, a 73 would have tied. I had some such lesson each year until I finally decided that the best of them made mistakes just as I did.

The advice Harry Vardon is supposed to have given, to keep on hitting the ball no matter what happens, is the best in the long run. It is useless to attempt to guess what someone else may do, and worse than useless to set a score for yourself to play for. A brilliant round or a string of birdies will not always win a championship. The man who can put together four good rounds is the man to watch.

No man can expect to win at every start. Golf is not a game where such a thing is possible. So the plan should be to play one's own game as well as possible and let the rumors and cheers fly as thick as they will.

The best competitive golfers are, I think, the distrustful and timorous kind, who are always expecting something terrible to happen—pessimistic fellows who are quite certain when they come upon the green that the ball farthest from the hole is theirs.

This kind of player never takes anything for granted and cannot be lulled into complacency by a successful run over a few holes. The most dangerous spot, where the cords of concentration are most likely to snap, comes while everything is going smoothly; when the hold upon concentration is a bit weak anyway, there is nothing like prosperity to sever the connection.

Over the Hill Course of Augusta Country Club in the second round of a tournament once, I got off to a shaky start. After collecting two 5's on the first two holes, the ball started rolling for me. The two strokes lost to par on the first two came back at the seventh and eighth; an additional one was gained at the eleventh, and another at the thirteenth, so that on the sixteenth tee I had par left for a 70. I had not made a costly mistake since the second hole and had left the difficult part of the course behind. Each of the last three holes was of drive-and-pitch length, probably the easiest stretch on the entire course.

Yet, although I did not realize it at the time, I allowed my attitude toward the rest of the round to become just what it should never have been. Seventy was good enough, I thought, and there was absolutely no danger of slipping a stroke on these last three holes. For me, the round was over; I had merely to go through the simple formality of holing out on 16, 17, and 18.

If I had been intent on picking up further strokes against par, as I should have been, I should have been far better off. If the finishing holes were such easy fours, why did I not attack them on the basis of threes? But I did not. I teed my ball on the sixteenth tee, addressed it carelessly, without even one look at the fairway, and hit a perfectly straight shot over the roadway out of bounds, and this too when confronted by one of the widest fairways of the course. The penalty being stroke and distance, I had thrown away two precious shots. That shocked me into consciousness again, and I called myself every kind of a fool I could 'think of, but that helped little toward getting the strokes back.

One shot carelessly played can lead to a lot of grief. I think a careless shot invariably costs more than a bad shot painstakingly played, for it leaves the morale in a state of disorder. It is easy to accept mistakes when we know that they could not have been avoided; we realize that many shots must be less than perfect, no matter how hard we try. But when we actually throw away strokes without rhyme or reason, it is pretty hard to accept the penalty philosophically, and to attack the next shot in the proper frame of mind.

I once heard of a man who, playing in the final of a club championship, had won his match on the last green after being two down and three to play. To accomplish this, he had played the last three holes in 5-4-5 against a par of 4-3-4. After the match, he had been congratulated most heartily upon his magnificent victory—snatching victory from defeat by a courageous finish, and all that.

Some weeks later during the same season this same man, over the same course, had reached the final of an invitation tournament. This time, instead of two down and three to play, he had found himself one up with three to play. He played the last three holes in par, 4-3-4, a stroke a hole better than on the previous occasion, yet this time he lost on the last green. Where his 5-4-5 had made him a hero, his 4-3-4 left him in shame, a creature of no backbone who faltered under the fire of competition.

And so it goes in golf. I have for this very reason an unspeakable aversion for the word "guts" as it is so often used in describing an attribute of a golfer. Not only has the ability to finish well, or to play golf at all for that matter, nothing in the world to do with physical courage, but it will be found that sensational recoveries and tragic failures are almost always accomplished by the cooperation of both sides.

3   CONSISTENCY

Everyone who has played golf, however well or badly, has found how impossible it is to hold his best form, or anything like it, for any length of time. A chart of a player's golfing fortunes over an extended period would exhibit a series of peaks and depressions, with the peaks very sharp, the downward curves precipitate, and the up slopes long and arduous. There is always a long struggle, painfully won, from the bottom of each valley to the top of the hill, and then, after a brief travel along the crest, the touch or feel that was so hard to find vanishes in an instant and back we go to the bottom.

There are two real reasons why absolute consistency is so rare in golf, and an appreciation of them will show something of what the golfer's problem is and will give him a chance to tackle it with his eyes open. The only two things that will ever enable him to smooth out the curve of his game chart are, first, a thorough understanding of the fundamentals of the swing, and, second, an intimate and unprejudiced acquaintance with his own faults and tendencies to fault.

A golfer must play by feel, and I know that I am not the only person who has found that no feel or conception, or idea, will work perfectly for very long. In other words, there is no one movement, or sequence of movements amenable to control, that being controlled, will continue indefinitely to produce satisfactory results. It is not possible to think through the entire swing when playing each shot. Sometimes by remembering to start the downstroke by shifting and turning the hips, highly satisfactory results may be obtained. While this continues, we are enjoying one of the peaks of our chart. But soon, either because we begin to exaggerate this one thing, or forget entirely about something else, the whole thing goes wrong and we have to begin over again. Again, we set out to find another thought that will set things right. This is the time when we need our understanding of the swing, for without this we shall be groping in absolute darkness.

The other reason why it is so hard to hold to form arises from the insidious nature of some of the faults that can creep into a golf swing without the player himself becoming aware of them. It has never been possible for me to think of more than two or three details of the swing and still hit the ball correctly. If more than that number have to be handled, I simply must play badly until by patient work and practice I can reduce the parts that have to be controlled. The two or three are not always the same; sometimes a man's swing will be functioning so well that he need worry about nothing; then, of course, on those rare occasions, the game is a simple thing.

But because we have not the capacity to think of everything while attention is directed elsewhere, a hundred little things can go wrong. Every year I played golf, I discovered more and more ways to miss shots, obscure and yet important mistakes I had never dreamed of making.

One important reason for the uncertainty of golf is that it is played over ground that in contour remains almost as nature shaped it. Hills and valleys, small mounds and undulations, deflect the ball this way or that. Two balls striking within a foot of the same place may finish yards apart—one in a bunker, the other near the hole.

One is inclined to overlook the times when a few feet more or less meant a difference of several strokes. When a ball stops a few inches short of a hazard, we seldom stop to think how lucky it was that it failed to roll in. Things of that kind occur on almost every hole of the course. They are regarded as merely parts of the game. It usually requires something almost startling to awake us to a full appreciation of the part actually played by the breaks of the game.

The first National Open Championship I won was saved for me by my ball taking a bound toward the hole instead of away from it, as it might well have done. Playing the sixteenth hole at Inwood in the last round of the championship of 1923, I was in the lead, but strokes were quite precious. After a good drive, I elected to play a number three iron to the green, which was protected by bunkers and mounds on either side, leaving a narrow opening in front. I must have felt the strain, for I wheeled the shot off to the left of the green, barely missing the bunker on that side, and watched it scamper into the roadway out of bounds. That meant the loss of stroke and distance, so I was playing 4 from the fairway.

Severely shaken by the mishap, I came very close to duplicating on the next shot the mistake that had cost me dearly on the first try. I remember wondering, as I watched the ball in the air, what I should do if that one, too, should go out of bounds. The ball came down on the side of the mound at the front of the green and, bounding almost at right angles, came to rest not over ten feet from the hole. I made the putt and so escaped with a 5 that ought to have been at least a 7. When I took 6 at the last hole, I was even more grateful for the lucky bound that enabled me to tie Bobby Cruickshank and remain with a chance for the championship.

When a fine drive goes sailing down the middle of the fairway, it is reasonable to expect that it will find at least a reasonably good lie. But when a wild shot goes off into the woods or rough, it is not likely to find an agreeable resting place.

When Walter Hagen and Leo Diegel came to the third tee on the number four course at Olympia Fields one afternoon, they were all even after thirty-eight holes of play. They were playing a semifinal match in the P.G.A. Championship. Diegel got away a fine drive down the narrow fairway. The course was fast, and he was left with a fairly easy second. Hagen, on the other hand, hit one of his wildest slices over a clump of trees and into what everyone knew was deep rough. Apparently, that ended the thing so far as Hagen was concerned. The situation of the green was such that a shot from the position of Hagen's ball would be almost impossible if it were found in long grass.

Most of the gallery scampered over the hill, anxious to see what Hagen could do in the way of extricating himself from a bad situation. But on arriving there, they found that Hagen was by no means out of the match yet, for instead of long grass, his ball had found a perfect piece of turf in a nursery kept to supply patches for the greens.

A fine iron shot put him on the green in 2 and the hole was halved in 4. Diegel was shaken by the surprise of that half and topped his drive on the next hole. There was no nursery waiting for him, so Hagen won the match.

Whatever may be a player's skill, he must have luck to win a championship of any kind—at least, he must have no bad luck; golf is still a game, rather than a science, and a game it is likely to remain. Possibly the feature of uncertainty is the chief reason for its popularity among players and spectators alike. One can never tell when the thrills will come thick and fast.

In seeking an explanation of the startling things that happen, one must appreciate that golf is a game requiring perfect coordination between mind and muscle—at least to the extent that a harassed mind will not prevent the muscles from performing according to long-established habit—and that in any field the margin enjoyed by any one of at least ten players can be only the difference in being on form or slightly off.

If any proof is needed that these sudden collapses are caused by the interference of fear and anxiety, numbers of instances can be cited in which players apparently out of the running, and so, relieved of the strain and the overwhelming responsibility, have gone back to playing free and easy golf and won championships. It is a fact that the winner of an important championship rarely starts out in the lead, holding it straight through to the finish without once being overhauled. Time after time, it has happened that the ultimate winner has begun his last round two, three, or four strokes behind the leader, and often playing early and almost unattended, has posted a low finishing round and a total score the others could shoot at in vain.

One of the most striking examples of the effect of the sudden relief that can come with disaster was furnished by Al Espinosa in the same National Open Championship at Winged Foot where I had one of my shocks. Al and I finished with the same seventy-two-hole total, but we compiled it in vastly different ways.

I started the last round with a lead, and even the two 7's that hit me on the eighth and fifteenth holes were never enough to put me so far down that I could be counted out. They just kept me in hot water. But Al started with a deficit to make up, and his play for ten holes, though not good enough to make up much ground, was yet sufficiently good to keep him up near the front where he could feel the pressure. Then the thing blew up all at once and he took an eight on the eleventh hole. Of course, everybody, including Al, knew that this was the finishing touch. He was the first of the leaders to come around, so he had no idea that the rest of us would have as much trouble as we did. Already a few strokes behind, he had dropped four more on one hole, and so, with only a few holes left, he thought he was definitely out.

And so he would have been if he had played par golf on the remaining holes. But the 8 that would have come close to paralyzing him if he had held a lead of two or three strokes was a relief for him in his actual position. With no thought now of winning, he started out to play golf, to hit the ball freely and in the old accustomed way. Four 4's and two 3's, two under par over six really tough finishing holes, and he had a score that landed him in a tie for the championship.

One newspaper writer said that this tournament was a contest to see who could throw away the championship the greatest number of times. It did look that way, but every championship is like that to some extent. Over the long stretch after the race has really settled down, the burden continually shifts from one man to another. The early leader falters under the strain; one behind, who has had no lead to protect and nothing to worry about, forges to the front, the strain gets him, and another takes his place. Troubles may come early, or late, or in the middle. But they all have them sooner or later.

4 EIGHTEEN-HOLE MATCHES

I admit, as some have urged, that eighteen holes constitute a round of golf. But since this came about by accident rather than design, the fact supplies no reason why eighteen holes should be accepted as an adequate test in important competition.

As a matter of fact, a definite superiority of one player over another, evidenced by performance over a long period of time, when expressed in terms of strokes per round, often must be noted in fractions. Open championships over seventy-two holes are rarely won by more than one or two strokes, yet certain men have shown an ability to win them with something approaching regularity. If a definite margin can exist, and yet be so small, a succession of short matches cannot possibly meet the requirements of a true test of ability.

I don't know yet how to regard eighteen-hole matches in a championship. I think it largely depends upon how the public, the press, and the players look at it—what importance they attach to the competition. Certainly, if the tournament is intended to determine the best golfer as champion, eighteen-hole matches defeat that aim. On the other hand, if it is intended only to be a pleasant week of golf to provide fun for the players and excite-

ment and thrilling finishes to watch and read about, then eighteen-hole matches are ideal. Somehow, I have never been able to
treat championships that lightly. They are not like invitation tournaments, and I don't think they ought to be.

In my day, I had no doubt that the British Amateur Championship was the most difficult to win of all the important prizes.
Starting with a big field that was not even reduced by stroke
qualifying rounds, a succession of eighteen-hole matches was played
all the way through to the final, which match alone was always
played at thirty-six holes; a man might be required to win seven
or eight short snatches in order to get his chance over the longer
route. Since there were always in the field any number of players
of little reputation who could nevertheless produce some devastat-
ing golf on occasions, upsets could always be expected. The full
week of the British Amateur could be a harrowing period for a
favorite. I always wanted to see how a top professional would enjoy the ordeal.

CHAPTER THIRTEEN

1 CONCENTRATION 211

2 COORDINATING THE SWING 214

3 GAINING EFFICIENCY 217

4 CONFIDENCE 219

5 STAYING ALERT 221

6 ANYTHING CAN HAPPEN 224

The Finish

CHAPTER THIRTEEN

I   CONCENTRATION

Playing on the National Golf Links, on Long Island, long ago, I happened to be driving very well. Alec Girard, the club professional, walking around with us, asked if there was any one thing I thought about that enabled me to keep on hitting the ball where I wanted it. I replied that when I was hitting the ball well, there were always one or two things I made certain of doing, and the doing of them would assure success for a while. But they were not always the same things. One conception was good for only a limited time, and when the charm wore off, I would have to begin looking for something else. Alec said emphatically that his experience had been the same.

This is something our theorists and analysts overlook when they are not themselves reasonably capable players. It is of great value to have a clear understanding of the successive movements making up a correct golf swing; this much is needed in order to enable one to recognize and correct faults as they appear. But no human is able to think through and at the same time execute the entire sequence of correct movements. The player himself must seek for a conception, or fix upon one or two movements concentration upon which will enable him to hit the ball. Then when this wears out, because perhaps he begins to exaggerate or overemphasize it to the detriment of something else, the search must begin anew for another idea that will work. In this process, there inevitably are alterations in the swing, not in fundamentals of course, nor of radical proportions, but more than can be accounted for in any series of diagrams.

If the expert player, possessing a swing that is sound in fundamentals, has to be continually jockeying about to find the means of making it produce fine golf shots, what of the average golfer who has never developed such a swing? Still groping for some sort of method that will give him a measure of reliability, it is only natural that he should try almost anything; and he must.

There is a lot in knowing what to tinker with and what to leave alone. In making day-to-day adjustments, I never considered even for a moment making any alteration, however slight, in my grip. It is of the utmost importance that the hands should be placed on the club so that they can perform certain necessary functions, and the correct grip should be the first thing learned. But after this has been done, the accustomed feel of the club should never be altered. It is only through the grip that the player is able to sense the location of the club head and the alignment of the face. If he is constantly changing here, he cannot possibly retain this feel. The temptation is great sometimes to try to correct a temporary hooking or slicing tendency by shifting the right hand more over or under the club. This should never be done. If the grip is wrong, change it by all means, but let the change be a permanent one.

The stance can vary considerably, shifting the feet to favor a hook or a slice; the ball can be shifted about within ample limits with respect to the feet. These little changes are by no means fundamental. Even what might didactically be prescribed as the correct swing allows some latitude in these matters.

The important thing the non-golfing theorist or analyst can seldom appreciate is the importance of the player's conception of how to put the correct swing to work. Very often what a man feels he is doing is more important than what he does. The feel, the experience, is so much easier to remember and repeat. When you arrive at a feeling of doing something in any part of the stroke and that something continues to produce good results, you will have a player's conception to hang onto. It is something upon which to concentrate, and this everyone must have in order to play consistent golf. Even the soundest swing must have some simple control to keep it in order.

To say that any round of golf offers a magnificent gamble in the way of form is to add nothing new. We all realize that we can never know in advance how the shots will go on a particular afternoon. To go even farther, we can have no assurance, after hitting seventeen fine tee shots, that the eighteenth will not be disgraceful. These are the uncertainties the golfer accepts as parts of the game, and indeed loves it all the more because of them.

Yet a player's satisfaction with the game he produces is measured directly by his ability to eliminate these bad shots and to correct the faults that inevitably find their way into his swing. In this one respect, at least, all golfers are on common ground, for in consideration of their respective skill and expectations, the problems of prevention and correction are the same for the dub and the expert.

Leaving entirely aside the question of skill and assuming that each individual has a standard to which he might reasonably expect to live up, perhaps it would be worthwhile to try to assign a reason for periodic or repeated failures to attain this standard. Of course, viewed in this way, the mechanical and physical sides are left entirely out. We want to know not why John Smith cannot play as well as Sam Brown but why John Smith so often fails to play as well as John Smith ought to play, with whatever skill he may possess.

Obviously, having eliminated every other variable, there is only John Smith's mind to look into, and this is where John Smith should look more often.

To play any golf shot correctly requires an unwavering concentration. The most perfect swing in the world needs direction, and plenty of it, and when its possessor begins to do a little mental daisy picking, something always goes wrong. A perfect attunement of every faculty is a thing even the finest players attain only very rarely, but by constantly keeping a vigilant watch over themselves they are able to shut out major vices over a comparatively long period of time. Their concentration is not occasional, but extends to every single shot, no matter how simple it may appear.

But human fallibility makes an unwavering concentration impossible, and this makes the commission of error unavoidable. The first lapse often leads to a second, and so on, until the whole structure is undermined and confusion results. The poor victim soon becomes unable to find anything to concentrate on. It is then that he must save himself by his knowledge and understanding of the swing, not necessarily of the perfect swing, but of his own. In order to have a chance of making progress, he must know, or have some idea, at least, of the sense of feel he is trying to regain.

Naturally, it is better to keep out faults than to have to correct them after they have made their appearance. Therefore, the longer a satisfactory concentration can be maintained, the better. But one thing may well be accepted at the outset, that as long as one continues to play golf, the happy periods will be followed by sorrow, and every swing will have to have periodic overhaulings.

But proper concentration during a round of golf is intended to accomplish something different from the perfect execution of each stroke. Powers of concentration alone cannot make up for any vast deficiency of skill and bring a mediocre player up to the level of one who possesses more real ability. But while on their respective form and ability to make shots and keep on making them, a wide gulf separates the champion from the average golfer, still, in one respect, their problems are the same when they start upon a round of golf. What each wants is a good round for him, and this leaves a comparison of their expectations entirely out of the issue.

2   COORDINATING THE SWING

It is surprising how easy it is to lose sight of the very obvious fact that in golf the all-important necessity is that the ball should be struck truly. It has often been pointed out, in connection with putting particularly, that the best judgment in the world and the most careful consideration of hazards and other dangers, are of little avail if the shot be not well struck. But to a greater or less degree, depending upon the skill and confidence of the individual, every golfer on earth suffers from this disturbance of his concentration, by influences entirely outside his own swing. I myself admit to equal guilt with the rest, although I have asked myself time after time if I derived any benefit from worrying about a hazard once I had decided upon the kind of shot to be played.

This is one of the reasons why the golf swing cannot be learned in actual play. No one can entirely ignore the responsibilities attendant upon the playing of any shot in a round of golf, no matter how unimportant may be the issue. Habits should be formed and instruction had on a practice tee where there is nothing to think about but hitting the ball.

Because no two men present the same appearance when striking a golf ball, and because nearly all instruction is along the same general line, the average observer may receive the impression that the expert does not practice what he preaches.

Many people I am sure have this idea. They feel that the pro has nothing to think of except hitting the ball, and that when he says he does so and so, he is merely guessing. Styles and mannerisms in a golf stroke are as varied as human appearances. To an experienced observer, it is just as easy to recognize a man by his swing as by his face, his back, or his gait. Yet mannerisms must not be confused with the fundamentals of the stroke. While Hogan may be easily distinguishable on the links from Player, yet there are certain basic principles both observe, and it is this basic swing with which teaching is solely concerned.

There are numbers of very fine golfers who give little thought to the details of the stroke and who make no effort to understand and prepare for the little troubles which may arise without warning. To these men, playing a golf shot is a sort of haphazard proposition to be performed either badly or well as chance may decide. They have not the ability to play consciously, for they do not know what direction to give to any control they may attempt to exercise. A fine natural swing is best let alone so long as it is in first-class working order; but no matter how sound the mechanism, there always comes a time when little adjustments have to be made; and it seems to work out that on the days when it is most necessary that everything be clicking, someone will loosen a nut, or forget to put in the oil, and everything will go to smash. Often, too, the strain of competition is a force sufficent to destroy a player who has played very well during the preliminary practice.

A fine swing with no knowledge or control of fundamentals may be enough to win occasionally. But it can be written that the consistent winner is aware beyond mere guesswork of what he is doing. To win consistently, or to be always near the top, requires that a man play well even when his swing is out of tune. Competitions cannot be arranged to find each player at the crest of his game. If the unlucky one cannot discover and surmount the difficulties, he will be left behind.

To play subconsciously considerably lessens the nerve strain of competition. More than that, it is usually the most effective way to play when the swing is in groove. Almost anyone can distinguish himself when these requirements are met. But the man at the top cannot afford to depend upon any such chance; he must be able, when anything goes wrong, to control the stroke consciously and direct it in such a way that good, sound golf will result.

True it is that on occasions the man with a good, sound swing can play good golf without giving much thought to the swing. On such occasions, he is able to sense a perfect coordination among all parts of his swing, and he knows it is right and is best left alone. When this happy state exists, the game is simple, the shots come off easily, and a fine score results with hardly any effort or worry.

But the unfortunate part of it is that this happens only very rarely, only a few times a year, and it comes and goes entirely apart from the will of the player. If Palmer, Player, Nicklaus, or any other golfer similarly equipped were able to arrange his perfect days to coincide with the Open Championship dates, he would be champion every year and have no need to know anything about his swing. Since he cannot do this and must make his effort in whatever state he finds himself, he must have a fairly accurate idea of how a correct swing can be accomplished.

A haphazard player may succeed once or twice if he happens to strike one of these inspired streaks at the right time. But in order to win or make a good showing consistently, he must be able to play good golf even when the inspiration has escaped him and he must work for what he gets. I think it may be taken that any player who is able to give a good account of himself in tournament after tournament knows pretty well how he is swinging the club and is able to think about his method while he is playing the shot. It ought to be perfectly plain that if he did not have these qualities, any tendency to error suddenly developed in the course of a round would have to go uncorrected and would prove disastrous.

Only in some such way as this is it possible to explain the fact that so many players, who are wolves in informal rounds, become lambs when faced by a card and pencil. Obviously, these men must know how to swing a golf club or they would not be able to play consistently well, no matter how informally; but the importance of a big tournament produces so great an anxiety in their minds concerning the result of a stroke that they cannot concentrate properly upon the making of it. They are not able to shut the prospect of failure from their minds long enough to complete the stroke without some sort of interruption, either of mind or nerve.

3   GAINING EFFICIENCY

Often, when we are trying to take strokes off our score, we attach too much importance to new theories of the swing, and overlook the fact that we are not getting everything we should out of the mechanical ability already possessed. Good golf, like any other human endeavor, is dependent upon human efficiency, and this is determined exactly as in the case of a steam engine, and is fixed by the percentage of latent power or ability that can be turned into effective work. The elimination of waste power, and the turning of every force to advantage, is the secret of high efficiency.

Every golfer is of limited ability—some more so, others less. We can't always help this, but I believe that I can make a few common sense suggestions, having nothing to do with technique, that will help to take strokes off any man's game.

The first real big lesson I learned, and it was medal competition that taught me, was that every stroke in the round was of equal importance, and that each one was worthy of and demanded the same intensity of concentration. Before I had had much experience, I used invariably to allow myself to become careleess when confronted by a simple-looking shot. A wide fairway or a big green was always the hardest for me to hit. But no golf shot is easy unless it is played with a precise and definite purpose, and with perfect and complete concentration upon results. The easiest way to assure minute attention on every shot is to cultivate an attitude of mind that will be satisfied by nothing less than perfection. If it looks easy to play onto the green, then try to get close to the hole; if it looks easy to get within a ten-foot radius, try to lay it dead. Always strive to go as far toward the ultimate end of holing out as it is reasonably possible to go.

The surest way to collect 7's and 8's and to pile up a disgraceful score is to become angry and rattled. It won't cost much in the way of strokes, when you slice a drive or pull an iron, if you throw your club away or curse your luck, because you still have time to get over it before the next shot. But if you look up in the bunker and leave your ball sitting where it was, you had best think twice before you hit it again.

No virtue in this world is so often rewarded as perseverance. Again, as Harry Vardon said, "Keep on hitting the ball." Don't give up just because you are bunkered in 3 and your opponent is on the green in 2. You might hole out and he might take three putts. It doesn't happen often, but you can never tell.

I used to be a very rapid player. But at Merion in 1925, I discovered that I was missing many shots simply because I was hitting the ball too quickly after I had reached it, especially on the putting green. Having walked up to the green at a brisk pace, and elbowed my way through whatever gallery there might have been, I had been putting quickly while my breath was coming in short gasps and my ears ringing as I leaned over the ball.

Realizing that I was making a mistake, I resolved that no matter how much time I consumed, I was going to tranquilize my breathing before I made another putt. So I began to take great pains to study the line. I really did not study the line, for I have never been able to see more rolls and bumps in a minute than I could in five seconds, but I was giving my breathing a chance to quiet down. You have no idea what a steadying effect upon the nerves can be had by doing some little thing in a natural manner. Light a cigarette, pick up a twig, or anything to take up a little time.

And that applies equally to shots through the green. Don't hit the ball until you are ready, until every other consideration has been excluded from the mind.

Another thing that often helps: When you have located the line to the hole and addressed the putt, often something gets blurred and you lose the line. Don't go ahead and putt anyway, for you must surely miss. Step away and start over again. You don't have a chance at first; you might make it the second time.

To those who play it and study it, the game of golf presents puzzling problems in many phases. One of the queerest angles on the mental side is seen when we begin to consider confidence—what is its effect, how much of it ought we to have; and in what should we have confidence—in our ability to beat a given opponent or in our ability to play the shots? Many of us have found that we can't play well without confidence of one kind, and that we will be beaten if we have too much of another variety.

4   CONFIDENCE

Every golfer has a favorite club—a battered old spoon or a mashie with a crooked shaft—that he would not exchange for double its weight in gold. He has confidence in this club and in his ability to use it; and in actuality, he does play it better than any other. It isn't all imagination—he doesn't merely think he can play it better—he can really do so because he has confidence in it and swings it easily, freely, and rhythmically.

The better player has this same feeling of confidence, but instead of trusting one of his clubs, he trusts them all, except perhaps one. He has confidence in his swing. He is content to trust himself to take his time and hit the ball. Such an attitude is indispensable to first-class golf.

It doesn't help a great deal to have the soundest swing in the world if that swing is not trusted. There are many men who play golf exceptionally well when the issues are small, but who collapse when anything of importance is at stake. The fact that they can play well at all shows that fundamentally their swings are good. But what causes the detonation is fear—lack of confidence in the swing—making them unwilling to trust it with anything that really matters. In the face of such an obstacle, tension takes the place of relaxation and strain upsets rhythm. The smoothest machine in the world cannot run in a bearing full of the gravel of uncertainty.

There is one kind of confidence that everyone must have in abundance; when he stands up to the ball ready to make a decisive stroke, he must know that he can make it. He must not be afraid to swing, afraid to pivot, afraid to hit; there must be a good swing with plenty of confidence to let it loose.

The other kind of confidence is a different thing, and a dangerous one. In a way, it has something to do with the player's opinion of his ability to play the shots, but it works in an entirely different way. Of this kind of confidence, we must have only enough to make us feel as we step upon the tee with John Doe: "Well, John, you're pretty good, but I think if I play hard and well, I can just about beat you." It must be enough to overcome actual fear or to rout an inferiority complex, but it must not be sufficient to produce a careless, overconfident attitude.

Every successful competitive golfer has learned to adopt a certain humility toward an opponent or an Open Championship field. He knows that no matter how well he plays, there may be someone who may play even better. Therefore, although he may be supremely confident of his ability to drive well, play his irons accurately, and putt well, he still is a fool if he is confident of winning—that is to any greater extent than I have indicated. Confidence in the club, or the swing, or the shot, aids concentration because it banishes tension and strain; a too-great confidence in the result of a match or a tournament makes impossible the concentration and hard work required to win.

It is difficult to assign any definite degree of importance to the operation of the player's imagination that enables him to visualize the shot to be played before he has even drawn a club from his bag. It is difficult, too, to say how complete the picture should be. A golfer of long experience, taking one look at the flag, instinctively knows with what club or clubs he can make the distance. A further consideration of wind, ground, and hazards will supply other details such as trajectory, high or low, and the kind of shot, whether straight, fade, or draw. The necessary preliminary to the playing of any stroke is the decision upon the club and the kind of shot to play. The player, in effect, merely applies an imaginary result to the problem in order to decide how it will fit.

But when the decision has been made and it comes time to step up to the ball, this picture of grass and flag and bunkers must fade into the distance—not entirely, to be sure, but far enough so that the attention can be focused mainly upon swinging the club. The strength of the blow—how hard to hit—is determined almost wholly by instinct. The picture in the back of the head is the guide for this, as well as for the nicety of club-face alignment needed to propel the ball exactly for the flag. But beyond this, complete concentration must be upon the swing.

Even the most expert player finds only very rarely that he can trust his swing entirely to habit and instinct. At all other times, there are certain things he must watch—body turn, hip shift, wrist-cock, or whatnot. For him, there is no magic in the loveliest picture of what ought to be the result of his stroke. He knows that in order to produce this pleasing result, he must swing his club correctly, and that is the job to which his immediate attention should be directed.

5 STAYING ALERT

Lindbergh said that the hardest thing he had to do in crossing the Atlantic was to keep awake. When you stop to think about it, that seems reasonable enough. It is not so easy to understand why the hardest thing a golfer has to do is to keep awake—mentally.

I do not believe there is another sport that requires the uninterrupted, intense concentration of the mind demanded of a
golfer in competition with others of anything like equal skill. In
all other games, it is possible to take breathing spells without
risking too much. But in golf the unexpected can, and usually
does, happen with such startling suddenness that the unwary
person may be caught before he knows it. One lapse of concentration, one bit of carelessness, is more disastrous than a number
of mechanical mistakes, mainly because it is harder to bring the
mind back to the business in hand than it is to correct or guard
against a physical mistake recognized as soon as it appears.

The habit of correct swinging causes a great many of the
movements of the swing to be instinctive. But there are always
two or three things that have to be looked after actively all the
time. When this is appreciated, it is possible to understand what
it means, when playing a first-class championship round, to
concentrate upon the execution of some seventy-two golf shots
in a space of eighteen holes and over a stretch of upward of
three hours' time.

And by concentration, I mean the kind that not only excludes
everything foreign to the game, but also takes account of all that
the player knows should be provided for. We find numbers of
players with fine form who hit the shots as well as anyone, yet
fail to win because of imperfect concentration. It is so easy to
walk up and hit the ball without thinking much about anything,
and the player never realizes until the damage is done that he
has not had his mind on the shot.

The men who are capable of complete concentration throughout an eighteen-hole round can be counted upon the fingers of
one hand. The others go to sleep on any number of shots. Sometimes they never realize even afterward that they did take a nap,
and often they mistake fear and anxiety for concentration. It is
possible to worry a great deal over the result of a stroke without
really thinking of the way to play it successfully.

This is one of the ways that mental staleness is manifested when
a player is overgolfed. The lack of mental alertness that results
renders it impossible for him to maintain complete concentration
on the details necessary to be considered for the different shots
he is called on to play. He is trying to the best of his ability,

but the thing is just beyond him, and he pays for it in the form of extra strokes on his score, or holes lost that might have been saved or even won with the right kind of keen mental application.

It might be asked again just what is concentration. I think that is very simple. There are certain fundamentals that go with every stroke. The right sort of concentration must take these into account. For example, the golfer should know that he should let the weight go with the swing; he should know also that he should turn the left side well around on the backswing. These are two things he should think about in advance of the swing, especially if he is troubled with a fault of overlooking these two points. He cannot take them for granted, they must be thought out before he starts his swing, and he must think through his current pattern of swinging to see that it is carried out, or at least concentrate enough to see that it is started on the way.

As I have said many times, the thing that makes a successful tournament player is not so much the ability to put in gear a swing that is not just right as it is the faculty for working good scores out of a game that is not tuned to perfection. It is largely a matter of experience and club manipulation, of getting the ball up there somehow with a shot that you know you can play, while you avoid as much as possible those that are uncertain. Golf tournaments don't just happen along when you and your swing are ready for them. You have to take them when and as they come and do the best you can.

For example, during the year 1926, I found myself utterly incapable of hitting a shot of any length in any way except with a fade, that is, from left to right. This was not my accustomed manner of playing. In fact during all the rest of my playing experience, I tended to favor the right to left, or drawing shot. Yet in this year 1926, simply by scrambling and maneuvering of the club and ball, I managed to win both the British and American Open Championships.

It is not easy for even the most experienced and golf-wise player to put his finger on a fault in his own swing and immediately apply a corrective. Often the period of struggling and searching runs into days and weeks. And then, as often as not, he finds that the trouble all came from some simple little thing that he knew perfectly well but had thought not worth checking up. Even granting that the rate of performance an expert has a right to expect is much higher than that to which the average golfer can aspire, certainly this is a cogent reason why the making of mechanical corrections should be postponed until after the round—that is, of course, if you are interested in the score you make.

Beyond forcing oneself to adopt this attitude, the only effort I should advise the average golfer to make when things begin to go wrong would be to think of rhythm, relaxation, and swinging. If he can avoid tightening up mentally and physically, if he can keep a cool head and refrain from hurrying his backswing, he can withstand almost any shock.

6 ANYTHING CAN HAPPEN

Illustrations of strange happenings in golf matches are not hard to find. Any of us can recall occasions when a trick of fortune either deprived us of a hole or an advantage seemingly secure or gave us a victory we in no way deserved. In such events, skill enters into the picture scarcely at all.

One such instance of startling effect occurred at Worcester in 1925 when Willie Macfarlane and I were playing off a tie in the National Open. In the first play-off, Willie had a lead of two strokes as we teed off on the fourteenth hole. Here he hit a beautiful tee shot, while I half-smothered mine. My ball failed to get out of the rough, and when I tried to use a spoon in an effort to reach the green, I sliced the shot badly into some more rough almost a hundred yards from the flag. When Willie pitched his second nicely on fifteen feet from the hole, my hopes appeared to be entirely gone. Already two down, I appeared certain of losing one, possibly two more strokes, which would have been the end, with only four holes left to play.

I was thinking about all this as I walked to my ball. I was

ready to give up. But my niblick pitch hit the green and rolled straight into the cup for a three. Willie, shaken perhaps, went for his putt, now to protect his lead rather than increase it, slipped a yard past and missed that one. I had gained two strokes instead of losing two, as I might have, and this enabled me to come out even in the first play-off, although Willie beat me in the later one.

Skill has almost nothing to do with a thing like that. Given this shot to play and one stroke in which to hole out, a ten- or twenty-handicap player would be almost as likely to make it as any professional. The hole-in-one reports prove this. A hundred average golfers make holes-in-one to each expert.

The mental attitude is important. One must keep on trying and keep on hitting the ball so that he may have a chance to enjoy a lucky break like this. But on the other hand, he must always be on guard lest his opponent surprise him with one of his own. Whether up or down, whether it is you in the bunker or the other fellow, anything can happen.

CHAPTER FOURTEEN

1 TAKING THE BREAKS IN STRIDE   229

2 PLAYING THE WIND   231

3 DIFFICULT CONDITIONS   232

4 EQUIPMENT   234

5 GOLF ARCHITECTURE   237

Putting

CHAPTER FOURTEEN

I TAKING THE BREAKS IN STRIDE

U phill and downhill lies, instances when the player must stand above or below the ball, close lies in swales and the like, when the ball must be gotten up quickly, these are the exacting situations of golf that offer opportunities for the skillful player to profit. At the same time, the certainty of frequent encounters with shots of this nature, in endless variety, accounts in large measure for the eternal fascination of the game.

It is for this reason, more than any other, that seaside terrain is regarded as the best for golfing purposes. There the undulating fairways furnish difficulties that bunkers do not provide, and, without punishing, call for the refinements of skill that an inland course rarely demands. Golfers who play these links learn to appreciate these difficulties and to enjoy trying to overcome them. Encountering lies of this kind so very often, they come to consider them desirable features of a proper course, instead of complaining of bad luck every time the ball is found in such a situation.

I think I first gained an understanding of this attitude upon my first visit to St. Andrews. Playing a practice round before the Open Championship with two American pros and a fellow member of the American amateur team of that year, we were accompanied by a small gallery of club members and townspeople, golfers all. I remember being puzzled when our shots from ordinary fairway lies were greeted with perfect silence, only occasionally broken by a discreet "well played" or "well done," when the ball stopped a little closer to the hole than usual. This was so dif-

ferent from the attitude of spectators in our own country. But
when one of us from a tricky lie brought up a shot with a spoon,
or brassie, our gallery became quite enthusiastic. Finally I realized that our golfwise friends were refusing to become excited
over what were merely good shots any first-class player would be
expected to make with some regularity. I suppose they figured we
would not have come so far to play in a championship if we could
not play these; but they were most appreciative of the skillful
execution of strokes of particular difficulty.

Incidentally, by cultivating the habit of accepting difficult lies as
part of the game, we can derive for ourselves more pleasure from
the playing of it. It will help us to remember that we tire of
banging balls from a practice tee, where for each successive shot
the lie of the ball and the problem is the same as for the preceding
stroke. We must have a change of scenery, but when we get too
much of it, we curse our luck.

One of the reasons Walter Hagen was such a great competitor
was his habit of accepting readily any problem the breaks of the
game may have tossed his way. Once a spectator, standing by
Walter's ball after it had taken a wicked kick into long grass, remarked to him as he came up that he had had bad luck. "Well,"
said Walter with a smile, "here it is and from here I have to play it."

The continual striving to improve our score, although entirely
natural, nevertheless does detract to some extent from our ability
to enjoy golf. When we become slaves to the card and pencil, we
become inclined to regard as total losses those rounds in which
our score mounts beyond our reasonable expectancy. When we
take pleasure in the game only according to the scorecard, a bad
start is likely to put entirely away the possibility of an enjoyable
afternoon.

The real way to enjoy playing golf is to take pleasure not in the
score, but in the execution of the strokes. A brassie shot to a green
can be just as interesting when played after a recovery from
trouble as when it follows a perfect drive. By cultivating this
attitude, one finally comes to welcome unusual situations, in which
there is the possibility of pulling off something a little out of the
ordinary. And again, such an attitude in itself brings better results
because it sustains interest and keeps one trying to the end.

2   PLAYING THE WIND

A competitive golfer has to put up with all sorts of weather and has to ride it through, for to take shelter during a medal round means instant disqualification. Through fourteen years of tournament play, I have seen at least my share, but I have never seen anything even remotely approaching that day at Sandwich playing for the St. George's Gold Vase. To the American players a dragon breathing fire, or anything else bearing a promise of warmth, would have been a welcome sight.

I remember my thoughts on awaking that morning and looking out from my window over a very turbulent English Channel and hearing the wind whistling under the sash of the window. I had heard of the boisterous weather of the Channel coast, but somehow I had not pictured it in connection with golf. Now the connection was becoming entirely too close for comfort.

Under ordinary conditions, or rather I should say, under conditions which we Americans regard as ordinary, St. George's is not an unusually difficult course. True, the first nine is tricky and deceiving and the second nine is rather long, but on the whole, scoring there is not a test of meticulous accuracy. But when the wind blows in true Sandwich fashion, the problem is something else entirely.

There were in the field this day all members of the American Walker Cup team, all members of the British team, and almost every other amateur of prominence in Great Britain. On the previous day, I myself, arriving for a practice round, had scored a 73 with little difficulty. Yet, of the fine field, 80 was the low score of the morning round and 78 of the afternoon, Major Charles Hezlett doing both and winning the medal.

I had always regarded with annoyance a wind of sufficient force to back up a tee shot twenty or twenty-five yards. Not only did the Sandwich gale blow the ball back at the player, but it made a problem of standing up long enough to hit the ball. The player was forced to lean against the wind in order to retain his balance, and during the swing, he felt that the club would be wrenched from his hands. I recall, as an example of the increased difficulty of playing, that the Sahara Hole, which we had all reached the day before with a drive and a three-iron, was played that day with a full drive, a shot up short of the vast bunker, a brassie across, and a chip or run-up to the green.

One really amusing thing happened to one of our players—I think it was Jesse Guilford—whose approach to the ninth green had come to rest shakily upon the crest of a ridge skirting the right edge of the putting surface. Jesse, preparing to putt, placed his putter on the turf behind his ball. The putter blade shut off the wind and the ball, starting to roll, continued into the rough. The putter had then to be exchanged for an eight-iron, a necessity that added not a bit to Jesse's enjoyment of the day.

A moderate wind provides a fine test of skill. The player who best controls his shot and displays the most resourcefulness in overcoming the difficulties imposed by the elements in windplay demonstrates a clean-cut superiority. But I am not sure that the same thing is true when a real gale is blowing. It seems to me then that the real test is of temperament rather than skill, the reward going to him who plods along unruffled and unexcited, refusing to become angry with himself or the results of his efforts. The man who can appreciate that 80 is a good score under such conditions is far ahead of the ambitious one who attempts to subjugate the elements and return his low 70's score in spite of them.

3   DIFFICULT CONDITIONS

It takes a great deal more than a good swing to get consistently good figures around the golf course. A good part of the game is played between the ears; meaning that judgment, based on thought and experience, is often as important as mechanical skill. Here are a few observations and suggestions I hope may be helpful in meeting some of the conditions of actual play not found on the practice tee.

A following wind tends to blow the backspin off the ball, to cause it to come down fast and run like a rabbit. If you are playing to a green with the wind at your back, you cannot rely much upon spin to stop the ball. Elevation is the only hope, and that isn't worth much unless the green has been soaked. It is best, when you can, to play the ball short and allow for the run. If you must pitch over a bunker or other obstacle, use a lofted club, not merely a club which will make the distance comfortably with the help from the wind, but one weaker than this, and hit the ball hard. If you are playing a short hole under these conditions, set the ball on a low peg tee. This enables you to get a cleaner contact, without the interference of grass, and gives you a better chance to get some spin that will hold.

The same is true when playing from a heavy lie in soft, green grass or clover. This shot also is difficult to stop and must be spanked hard with a lofted club. In either case, if the green is the least bit firm and closely bunkered, you are not likely to be able to hold it. But this is your best chance.

A head wind accentuates the backspin and tends to make the ball peak toward the end of its flight. A steep pitch into the wind is very difficult to control. This is the time to take a stronger club to keep the ball down. If you have anything like a clean lie, you can bang the ball all the way up to the hole with absolute assurance that it will sit down. You can almost stop a shot on concrete if you have a strongish breeze in your face.

The most common tendency toward slicing becomes greater as the face of the club becomes straighter. In other words, most players are more likely to slice, or likely to slice more with a straight-faced club than with one of greater loft. So, when the wind is blowing across the course from right to left, it is usually better to take a club a little stronger than is needed; and, conversely, when the wind crosses from the other side, a more lofted club and a full swing usually work better. Obviously, this cannot be precisely true in all cases. But this is the rule, according to my observation, and it helps a great deal to take cognizance of it.

This much, of course, concerns the shot to the green where it is control, rather than length, that is wanted. The ball that comes in with the wind will naturally roll more than the one that is turning its head into the current. Off the tee, many players ride the wind in order to gain length. For my part, it seems better to keep the ball in the fairway, rather than go out after a few extra yards. If you ever get off a bad hook or slice with the wind helping out, you may find your ball in the next county, if you find it at all.

As a final word, do not make too much of hitting the tee shots down into a head wind. When you hit the ball down, you give it backspin. It starts out low and looks very pretty and very expert, but the spin makes it climb or peak near the end of its flight and it drops almost lifeless. Even against the wind, the ball struck squarely in the back or a little bit up is the distance-getter. Such a shot keeps its head down and continues to bore in, and it has something left when it strikes the ground.

4   EQUIPMENT

A tall man does not necessarily require longer clubs than a short man. This problem is controlled by a number of factors, by the posture the player prefers, that is, by the degree of bend he finds most comfortable, by the distance from the ball he likes to maintain—and by the breadth of arc that gives him the best balance between distance and control. In short, the determining factor is comfort. There is no rule that so many inches of height requires so many inches of club.

Since the advent of the steel shaft, golf club lengths have been more or less standardized. It never was a good idea to alter the length of any kind of club that left the manufacturer's or club-maker's hands perfectly balanced. Such a procedure has become even less a good idea now, because the steel cannot be scraped or pared down to restore the feel destroyed by decreasing the length. But the necessity that the player balance length and control in the selection of a club has enabled the manufacturers of steel-shafted clubs to arrive at standard lengths that are suitable to almost all individuals. They could never have done this if it had been true that the length of the club had to vary in direct proportion to the length of the player.

Back in the times when everyone was using hickory, I remember being surprised upon discovering that Long Jim Barnes' driver was a shade shorter than my own, and some time later, upon learning that Wee Bobby Cruickshank's was some little longer. Evidently, in these cases the lengths of the clubs used by two men of almost a foot difference in stature had been brought to almost the same point by the balance of control and length. Barnes, with his great height, was able to get all the arc he could control with the shorter club, and Cruickshank needed a comparatively longer club to get distance.

Many men of short stature have experimented with abnormally long clubs. Cruickshank was one of these. There was one fine player in England who carried a fifty-inch driver, but he rarely used it because it was not easily controllable. I used to use long shafts in my irons, but cut them off in 1926 at Tommy Armour's suggestion, and found my iron play much improved.

I have rarely run across a club in any man's bag to which I could not accommodate myself, the lengths have been so little different from my own. But I regard this as a phenomenon that by no means alters the fact that shaft lengths are to be determined wholly on the basis of individual preference. My chief warning is to avoid the idea that height and reach, or either, are the controlling factors. Comfort is the main thing, and a tall man need not be surprised if he likes a short club, or a short man a long one.

Golf is throughout a game of compromises, in which it is always necessary to make sacrifices in one direction in order to gain, or to fail to lose, something of equal importance on the other side. Thus we are compelled to give up a certain amount of length for accuracy and control, of backspin for safety, and so on. Whenever we begin to measure the ultimate possibilities of any shot, we are always hauled back by an appreciation of the risks involved.

This, of course, any golfer recognizes. But what he does not see with equal clearness is that this necessity for compromise extends even to the ball he uses. The three desirable features of any ball— assuming all to be well made and therefore uniform and reliable— are length or power, durability, and feel. It so happens that after a certain point is past, no two of these factors can be enhanced except at the expense of the remaining one. Most manufacturers have recognized, because this is true, that the average golfer should have a ball different from one that fits the expert. But an imperfect understanding of just what can be built into a golf ball has prevented this from benefiting the average player as it should.

One may well begin with the positive assurance that no first-class ball is as much as twenty yards, or even fifteen yards, longer than any other first-class ball. This difference, on the driving machine, is rarely more than two or three yards on carry; by increasing compression, the advantage of one over the other can be stepped up to approximately six yards. But as the compression is stepped up by means of a tighter winding, and the driving power increased, the ball becomes less durable, easier to cut, and begins to have a harder, stonier feel.

The ball that is tightly wound, that is, is of high compression, is the ball for the expert. He can hit it hard enough to make use of its added power; and the feel of the ball can be softened somewhat by applying a thinner cover. The player who hits every shot on the nose, and rarely half-tops one, can afford to use such a ball. Often a difference of five yards on the drive, or ten yards in two full wood shots, will be very valuable. But the average golfer using this ball might require a new one every few holes, the tighter winding has added power, and the thinner cover has improved the feel, or at least offset the effect of the higher compression, but the durability factor has been reduced considerably. It is well to remember, too, that the difference of two or three or five yards mentioned before contemplates a carry of from 230 to 250 yards. For shorter lengths, it is considerably less.

With the size and weight of the ball standardized, its power can be increased in no other presently known ways. I think the average golfer might well ask himself if the game is worth the candle. Certainly, it would seem to me that he should prefer a combination of a somewhat lower compression and a more durable cover, even if the driving capabilities of the ball, which he will never reach anyway, were a few yards less. I think that most players are inclined, all the way through, in the ball, the club, and the swing, to assign too much importance to length at the expense of accuracy and reliability. It is far more important for them to use balls each one of which will respond in precisely the same way to every type of stroke.

At any rate, a better understanding of the possibilities of golf ball construction will enable each player to select with his eyes open the ball he prefers to use. Certainly, this is a decision he has every right to make for himself.

5 GOLF ARCHITECTURE

Almost every golfer cherishes an especial fondness for one particular golf course. Even when he does not stop to find the reason for it, he recognizes that he can derive more enjoyment from playing one course than another. It is the business of the designer and builder of golf courses to discover and to utilize the features that make the superior course more enjoyable.

It seems to me that many courses are designed with an eye to difficulty alone, and that in the effort to construct an exacting course that will thwart the expert, the average golfer who pays the bills is entirely overlooked. Too often the worth of a layout is measured by how successfully it has withstood the efforts of professionals to better its par or to lower its record.

The first purpose of any golf course should be to give pleasure, and that to the greatest possible number of players, without respect to their capabilities. As far as is possible, there should be presented to each golfer an interesting problem that will test him without being so impossibly difficult that he will have little chance of success. There must be something to do, but that something must always be within the realm of reasonable accomplishment.

From the standpoint of the inexpert player, there is nothing so disheartening as the appearance of a carry that is beyond his best effort and that offers no alternative route. In such a situation, there is nothing for the golfer to do, for he is given no opportunity to overcome his deficiency in length by either accuracy or judgment. The problem supposed to be offered him becomes no problem at all when he has nothing to look forward to.

Whenever there is a carry offered, two things are essential. First, there must be a way around for those who are unwilling to accept the risk, and there must be a definite reward awaiting the man who takes the chance successfully. Without the alternative route, the situation is unfair; without the reward, it is meaningless.

The ideal golf course would have to be played with thought as well as mechanical skill. Otherwise, it could not hold a player's interest. The perfect design should place a premium upon sound judgment as well as accurate striking by rewarding the correct placing of each shot. Mere length is its own reward, but length without control ought to be punished.

There are two ways of widening the gap between a good tee shot and a bad one. One is to inflict a severe and immediate punishment upon the bad shot, to place its perpetrator in a bunker or in some other trouble demanding the sacrifice of a stroke in recovering; the other is to reward the good shot by making the second simpler in proportion to the excellence of the drive. The reward may be of any nature, but it is more commonly one of three, a better view of the green, an easier angle from which to attack a slope, or an open line of approach past guarding hazards. In this way, upon the long, well-placed drive—possibly the one that has dared an impressive bunker—is conferred the greatest benefit, but shots of less excellence are still left with the opportunity to recover by bringing off an exceptionally fine second.

A course constructed with these principles in view must be interesting, because it will offer problems a man may attempt, according to his ability. It will never become hopeless for the duffer, nor fail to concern and interest the expert; and it will be found, like old St. Andrews, to become more delightful the more it is studied and played.

In a letter I once received from the Research Committee of the United States Golf Association Greens Section, the statement was made that: "We believe that much of the difficulty in maintaining putting greens is due to excessive use of water. The greenskeepers and greens committees point out that they do this in self defense because golfers all want soft greens." I was asked to say how I regarded the practice of keeping green surfaces soft, even soggy, looking at the question purely from the playing standpoint.

There can be little question that the great mass of golfers in this country prefer their greens very soft. Such a condition makes the play much easier for all classes of players, and is in great measure responsible for the fact that tournament scoring is uniformly lower over here than on seaside links in the British Isles. The difference is attributable more to this factor than to the much-talked-of seaside gales, which, after all, do not blow constantly.

I cannot say which induced the other, or which came first, but there is a close relationship between our two great American preferences, the one for placing our green-bunkering very close to the putting surfaces, and the other for soggy greens that will hold any kind of pitch, whether struck with backspin or not. The close guarding in many instances makes a soft green necessary if the hole is to be playable, and the easy pitching, on the other hand, makes it necessary to decrease the size of the target in order to supply any test at all.

I quarrel with both ends of this proposition, whichever is to blame. These together are the two reasons, I think, why our golf courses in the main lack the subtlety of British links, and why our golf does not demand the strategy or the intelligent planning that it should. In my opinion, a properly designed hole should impose a test upon each shot the player has to make. There should always be a definite advantage to be gained from an accurate and intelligent placing of the tee shot, or a reward offered for a long, well-directed carry over some obstacle. This advantage or reward can only be in the shape of an easier and more open road for the second shot. Yet when we soak the green with water, we nullify the advantage the design of the hole has held out.

I do not believe in forcing a run-up shot in preference to a ptich in every case. But when one goes to the trouble of placing a bunker across the left side of the green in order to force the tee shot toward the right side of the fairway, why destroy its effect by soaking the green so that any sort of pitch over the bunker will hold? Our expert players are in the habit of playing long iron and spoon and brassie shots bang up to the hole. As long as they can do this, no architect can expect them to worry much about placing tee shots.

It seems to me that the ideal green would be sufficiently soft only to hold a properly played pitch—and by "hold" I do not mean to stay within a very few feet. To carry out the intention of the designer, conditions ought to be such that a definite penalty should be sustained by the player who has played himself out of position.

In this connection, I think one of our greatest needs is a fairway grass or treatment that will make the ground in front of our greens more reliable. If the greens themselves are maintained in a firmer condition, the need must arise on occasions to drop the ball short of the putting surface, allowing it to roll the remaining distance. I know very few courses where this is possible without great uncertainty.

CHAPTER FIFTEEN

CONCLUSION

CHAPTER FIFTEEN

U P to this point, except for the first chapter, this book has presented the substance of my writings of thirty or more years ago, and the chief concern of these writings was to record my conception of the proper golf swing and of related considerations affecting the playing of the game. Now, briefly, I should like to offer my impressions of what has happened to golf in the past thirty years. My conviction is that this period has been most productive for the game.

I have no question that this period has produced some of the finest players in the history of the game. Record scoring has become commonplace, and the general level of skill among tournament performers has been consistently elevated. We see more and more fine players every year, and competition grows keener and keener.

In many respects, golf has become an easier game; greenskeeping methods have progressed; hybrid grasses more suitable for golf courses have been developed; there is a more widespread use of artificial watering; golf course designers have constructed many fine new courses, and modernized some of our old favorites. Resulting from all these influences, we have better fairways, more uniform and reliable putting surfaces, and courses that are generally more interesting to play. So it is with good reason that golf has become a more popular and attractive game.

It appears that there is today no longer the wide difference between inland golf in America and seaside golf in Great Britain. Since I wrote the chapter immediately preceding this one, there has been a considerable improvement in golf courses in this country.

Many of our new courses have greens of ample size, and greens-keepers are no longer under pressure to keep the turf of these greens in a sodden condition.

At the same time, it seems that turf conditions in Great Britain have come more nearly to approximate our own. On my visit to St. Andrews with the Eisenhower Cup team in 1958, the main difference I noted in the Old Course was an increased lushness in the turf. Formerly, the fairways had been quite fast and the greens more than firm; such conditions made necessary a kind of maneuvering entirely unfamiliar to American players. Now the fairway turf has more depth and the greens are more holding. From this observation, confirmed by correspondence with some of my friends on the other side, I have come to suspect that British seaside golf as we used to know it no longer exists.

Although in these past thirty years we have produced in this country more fine golfers than we have ever seen before, the United States is no longer supreme in the game without challenge; no longer either is the main force in the game divided been this country and Great Britain. South Africa and Australia especially are doing more than challenge; they are leading us at the moment on a merry chase. It would seem likely that other countries will before long move up to claim places for their players. All this I think is healthful for the development of the game.

In taking a hard look at modern golf, I find in the play from tee to green little difference indicating any considerable superiority of the present-day player over the dozen or so better players of my era. True, the tee shots are somewhat longer and the whole rate of performance through the green is somewhat more regular. I attribute much of this to the steel shaft, but also a good measure to the fact that the tournament players of today play in many more competitions; even the professionals in my day were mostly occupied with club jobs during the summer months.

On the other hand, once we have reached the putting surface, the modern golfer becomes a magician. I never dreamed I should see the kind of putting our tournament players are now producing. Whereas we used to consider an average of 32 or 33 putts per round to represent a quite acceptable performance for the winner of a championship, now it is not uncommon to see this number reduced to 28, 27, or even occasionally to 26. The resulting effect upon scoring is obvious. At times, I find myself mildly, even though enviously, amused by the agonies expressed before television cameras when some players fail to hole out from 25 or 30 feet. Most of my contemporaries were well pleased if from such distances they could consistently roll the ball close enough to the cup to make certain of holing the next one.

It may well be that improved putting surfaces are factors here, but I believe a far greater contribution is made by the increased putting skill of the players themselves.

The one thing I do not like about modern golf, especially the tournament variety, is the frequency with which balls are lifted and cleaned on the putting surface. It used to be a fundamental principle of the game of golf that a ball put in play from the tee should not be touched until it was removed from the hole; departures from this principle were to be made only with very good reason. One such reason, of course, in stroke or medal play was to remove interference with the play of a fellow competitor. But players were always careful when lifting a ball for this purpose to take precaution to replace it in the precise position from which it had been lifted, so that any mud or other material clinging to the surface of the ball would remain as it had been. A ball lifted from another competitor's line of putt was not to be placed into the player's pocket nor rolled on the ground, but held carefully in the fingers until replaced.

With the fine conditioning of our modern courses, I doubt that troublesome mud would be picked up by many balls. Unusual conditions of ground or weather could be cared for by special rules. The elimination of constant lifting and cleaning would speed up the game to the benefit of players and spectators alike.

I am tempted at this point to unburden myself of some appraisals of the great players of these last three decades, but I know all of them so well and have such a high regard for their capabilities and their pride in their accomplishments in the game that in the end I cannot bring myself to say that one or two could be better than the others. In any case, such an expression would only be one man's opinion on a question that necessarily is so close as to require the splitting of a hair. Let us just say that we should be greateful for the contributions all have made and realize that even though the top players have reaped rich rewards from their skill, they have also provided for the game an immense stimulus that has made it a much more enjoyable and attractive pastime for the average golfer, who, after all, is the guy—or bloke, or whatever you choose to call him—who supports the game.